COMMEMORATIO BREVIS
DE TONIS
ET PSALMIS MODULANDIS

Introduction, Critical Edition, Translation

by TERENCE BAILEY

THE UNIVERSITY OF OTTAWA PRESS
Ottawa, Canada
1979

COMMEMORATIO BREVIS
DE TONIS
ET PSALMIS MODULANDIS

ÉTUDES MÉDIÉVALES DE L'UNIVERSITÉ D'OTTAWA
OTTAWA MEDIAEVAL TEXTS AND STUDIES

This book has been published with the help of a grant from the Canadian Federation for the Humanities, with funds provided by the Social Sciences and Humanities Research Council of Canada.

Preface

Although the chanting of the psalms is central to virtually every service of the medieval liturgy, and although their musical tradition has roots which reach back to the very beginnings of Christianity, and beyond, documentation for the psalm tones in the earliest centuries is very scanty. It is perhaps the ubiquity of the psalms which explains the absence of written evidence: it is unnecessary to record what everyone knows by heart. The appearance of the *Commemoratio Brevis* [1] marks the beginning of the written tradition. This anonymous treatise is the oldest source for the Gregorian psalm tones, perhaps even the earliest musical document for Christian psalmody, and all the more valuable in that it records the melodies in a notation which is pitch-accurate. Moreover, it contains some of the clearest descriptions of the rhythm of Gregorian Chant in the early Middle Ages and important information on practical matters concerning the singing.

The value of the treatise is enhanced for scholars by another circumstance: the practice it describes was intended by the author to be universal in its application. Although it is safe to say that certain features of the psalm tones are of very great antiquity, [2] it was not until the twelfth or thirteenth century that there was anything like general agreement in the churches; it was not until recently, in the books of Solesmes, that all details of the Gregorian psalmody have been codified. Even the late medieval practice varied considerably, especially for the medians and terminations. Some communities maintained a large number of variations; [3] others, especially the more severe monastic orders, made do with a very few. [4] At the time of the *Commemoratio Brevis* the practice for the psalms must have been

---

[1] Fétis and Coussemaker, for no very good reason, decided that "Commemoratio" must be emended to "Commentatio." See E. COUSSEMAKER, *Mémoire sur Hucbald* (Paris, 1841), 89. Hucbald's authorship, accepted by Gerbert *(Scriptores Ecclesiastici de Musica Sacra Potentissimum* [St.-Blasien, 1784], I, 103), has long been abandoned. See Hans MÜLLER, *Hucbalds echte und unechte Schriften über Musik* (Leipzig, 1884).

[2] For an attempt at dating the various portions of the psalm tones see Amédée GASTOUÉ, "La psalmodie traditionnelle des huit tons," in the *Tribune de Saint-Gervais,* XIV (1908), 274.

[3] The *Liber Usualis* gives more than forty.

[4] See Michel HUGLO, *Les tonaires* (Paris, 1971), 392, 366.

that much more diffuse. The treatise itself refers to the diversity, accepting the situation with good grace *(30)*.[5] But the anonymous author has compiled his manual with the evident intention of providing a standard practice valid beyond the walls of the monastery in which it was written *(22)*, and in his work one may hear echoed the educational zeal of the Carolingians, the same concern for uniformity in the Liturgy which produced the astonishing agreement displayed by the earliest chant-books.

The importance of the *Commemoratio Brevis* has not gone unnoticed by scholars; nevertheless the only publication has been that of Gerbert in 1784.[6] Gerbert's edition contains numerous errors and some evident lacunae, defects which made it difficult for later writers such as Coussemaker, Petit, Wagner, Auda and Ferretti[7] to come to any clear understanding of the psalmodic practice the treatise contained. Ferretti, for example, was led finally to declare that the work was lacking in logic:[8]

> Le procédé que nous révèle la *Commemoratio Brevis* est absolument empirique et arbitraire.... Comment donc les Maîtres de Chœur s'y prenaient-ils pour obtenir l'ensemble indispensable entre les Chanteurs, cet ensemble tant recommandé par l'auteur de la *Commemoratio Brevis*? Mystère!

The faults of the Gerbert edition are not, for the most part, the result of carelessness by the great German scholar; the difficulties lay in his sources. Gerbert based his edition on a manuscript in the collection of his monastery at St.-Blasien. This manuscript (our P) is presently—along with Gerbert's proof-sheets for his edition—found at St.-Paul. It may be inferred from Gerbert's sketchy remarks in the *Scriptores*,[9] and perhaps from one or two of the readings of his edition, that he also examined one or both of the Paris manuscripts. He seems to have been unaware of any other sources.

It is not to be supposed that all the difficulties of the older edition have been resolved with the aid of readings from additional manuscripts. The treatise still has defects which only fresh sources could rectify, and a good deal of conjectural emendation has been necessary to make sense of its musical examples. But the *Commemoratio Brevis* in the present edition is clearer in intent, a more complete and reliable witness than has hitherto been available.

---

[5] These numbers refer to the text of the treatise.

[6] *Op. cit.*, 213.

[7] All of these authors (see the Bibliography) made transcriptions from Gerbert's edition. Some, like Wagner, attempted to emend obvious absurdities, but others, like Coussemaker (and even Ferretti) allowed quite preposterous readings to stand.

[8] *Esthétique grégorienne* (Paris, 1938), 315.

[9] GS I, 103.

Table of Contents

Introduction

THE MANUSCRIPTS

The *Commemoratio Brevis* has been transmitted in part or fully in the following manuscripts, which are the basis of the present edition.

Ba

    Barcelona, Archivo de la Corona de Aragón, MS Ripoll 42, eleventh century, from the monastery of Ripoll, parchment, 113 ff., 257 × 347 mm.

    For a complete description of this manuscript see Yves CHARTIER, *La "Musica" d'Hucbald de Saint-Amand*, Institute of Medieval Music (New York, to appear 1979). The first part of the Commemoratio Brevis (*explicit*: apud nos habet) is found on ff. 57v-58.

Bg

    Bamberg, Staatsbibliothek MS Var 1, tenth century, cf. Michel HUGLO, *Les tonaires*, 63, 66. Perhaps from Rheims, parchment, 66 ff.

    f. 2:   *Incipit Scolica Enchiriadis de Musica*
            Musica quid est ... retinet modum. *(GS I, 173-212)*

    f. 38v: *De Laudis Dei Disciplina Sermo*
            Hoc vero admonendum ... scienter deo obsequi.
            (i.e. from the Commemoratio Brevis)

    f. 40:   *Quod in Aliquibus Rationis Huius Profunditas Minus Sit Penetrabilis*
            Fictum est ab antiquis ... ponamus hic finem.
            (GS I, 172-3)

    f. 42v: *Incipit Commemoratio Brevis de Tonis et Psalmis Modulandis*
            Debitum servitutis nostrae ...
            Gloria seculorum amen. Euge serve bone.

    f. 47:   celi celorum laudate ... deuterum extat inconsonus.
            (GS I, 157-171)

    f. 59v: *Item de Diatessaron et Diapente ac Diapason et de Symphoniis*
            Triplica. divide maiorem ... laudibus ad plicandum.

f. 61:　　Superficies quaedam ... concordia aeterna coierit.
　　　　　(GS I, 171-2)
f. 61v:　*Item de Musica et de Ratione Eius*
　　　　　Musica partes sunt tres ... suscipit organale decus.
f. 64:　　*(hymn)* Rex Caeli domini *cum notis musicis*
f. 65:　　*De Cantu I Capitulum*
　　　　　Observandum est ut aequaliter ... legitur habeatur in
　　　　　manibus.

C

Cambridge, Corpus Christi College Library, MS 260, tenth
century, from Christ Church, Canterbury, parchment, 54 ff.,
270 × 189 mm.
For a description of this manuscript see M.R. JAMES, *A Descriptive Catalogue of the Manuscripts in the Library of Corpus Christi College Cambridge* (2 vols, Cambridge, 1911-12), II, 10.
The opening of the Commemoratio Brevis (*explicit*: deuterum
excellentem) is found on ff. 51v-53v.

J

Cracow, Biblioteka Jagiellońska, MS 1965, late eleventh or early
twelfth century, probably from northern Italy, parchment,
116 pp., in 4to. Cf. HUGLO, *Les tonaires*, 69. For a complete
description of this manuscript see Chartier, *La "Musica."* The
beginning of the *Commemoratio Brevis (explicit*: apud nos
habet) is found on pp. 59-60.

M1

Munich, Bayerische Staatsbibliothek, Clm 14649, late tenth
century or early eleventh, from St.-Emmeran, Regensburg,
parchment, 67 ff., in 4to.
f. 1:　　*two musical charts*
　　　　　1)　string lengths and pitches
　　　　　*2)　the relative positions of the plagal and
　　　　　　　authentic ranges*
f. 1v:　*Incipiunt Quaedam Utiliora de Arte Musica Scolica
　　　　　Enchiriadis Liber I*
　　　　　Sicut vocis articulate ... retinet modum.
　　　　　(GS I, 152-212)
f. 32v:　*Incipit Commemoratio Brevis de Tonis et Psalmis
　　　　　Modulandis*
　　　　　Debitum servitutis nostrae ... apud nos habet.
f. 33v:　Super unum concavum lignum ... tetrachordo notabilis.
f. 34v:　*Ecce Modorum Sive Tonorum Auspice Christo Incipit
　　　　　Ordo*

Primus tropus habet ... verum cantilenae corpus.
(GS I, 124-5)

f. 35v: *(not concerned with music)*

M2

Munich, Bayerische Staatsbibliothek, Clm 14272, mid-eleventh
century, from St.-Emmeran after a Chartres model, Regensburg,
parchment, 192 ff. Cf. HUGLO, *Les tonaires*, 253.

f.1: BOETHIUS, *De Musica*
f. 62: Tonary
f. 65: *(not concerned with music)*
f. 155: *Incipit Liber Enchiriadis de Musica*
        Sicut vocis articulate ... ponamus hic finem. *(GS I, 152-73)*
f. 161: *Incipiunt Scolica Enchiriadis de Arte Musica*
        Musica quid est ... retinet modum.
        (GS I, 173-212)
f. 173v: *Incipit Commemoratio Brevis de Tonis et Psalmis Modulandis*
        Debitum servitutis nostrae... in deuterum excellentem.
f. 174v: Super unum concavum lignum ... tetrachordo notabilis.
f. 175: *Alia Musica*
        De harmonica consideratione ... tonum octavum require ut supra. *(GS I, 125-147)*
f. 181v: *(not concerned with music)*

P

St.-Paul (Kärnten), Klosterbibliothek, MS 29.4.2 (132/6), late
tenth century or early eleventh, from St.-Blasien, parchment,
9ff., 235 × 315 mm.

f.1: *Incipit Commemoratio Brevis de Tonis et Psalmis Modulandis*
      Debitum servitutis nostrae... deo obsequi.
f. 9v: a chart of the echematic formulas in daseian and
       neumatic notation. *(GS I, 229)*

An older foliation, visible at the top, centre, reveals that this
manuscript formed, at one time, ff. 159-167 of a larger codex.
This manuscript is the source of Gerbert's edition.

P1

Paris, Bibliothèque Nationale, MS lat. 7212, eleventh or twelfth
century, from Luxeuil, parchment, 52 ff., 335 × 230 mm. For a
complete description see J. SMITS VAN WAESBERGHE, *The
Theory of Music* I (Munich, 1961), 105 (Cf. HUGLO, *Les tonaires*, 156, n.1). The beginning of the *Commemoratio Brevis*
(explicit: deuterum excellentem) is found on ff. 36-37v.

P2

Paris, Bibliothèque Nationale, MS lat. 7211, ff. 1-72v from the thirteenth century, ff. 73-151v from the early twelfth, from the SW of France, parchment, 151 ff., 280 × 180 mm.
For a complete description see J. Smits Van Waesberghe, *The Theory of Music* I (Munich, 1961), 101. (Cf. Huglo, *Les tonaires*, 68). The first part of the *Commemoratio Brevis* (*explicit*: deuterum excellentem) is found on ff. 49-51.

W

Wolfenbüttel, Herzog-August-Bibliothek, MS 4376 (72 Gud. lat. 2°), late tenth or early eleventh century, from the monastery of Sts Ulrich and Afra in Augsburg, parchment, 88 ff.
For a description of this manuscript see O. Heinemann, *Die Handschriften der Herzoglichen Bibliothek zu Wolfenbüttel* IV. (Wolfenbüttel, 1913), p. 124.
The *Commemoratio Brevis* is found on ff. 82v-87. A chart of echematic formulas (GS I, 229) is found on the last page.

THE RELATIONSHIP OF THE MANUSCRIPTS

The fact that so many of the manuscripts of the *Commemoratio Brevis* are fragments—some very brief—makes it impossible to establish their filiation in any great detail. The evidence allows only a few general conclusions and some more or less likely conjectures. First of all, on the basis of textual variants as well as length, the manuscripts may be grouped as follows:

1) the Wolfenbüttel and St.-Paul MSS (W P)
2) the Bamberg MS (Bg)
3) the four manuscripts which terminate with "in deuterum excellentem" (C M2 P1 P2)
4) the three manuscripts which terminate with "apud nos habet" (Ba J M1).

With respect to any further relationships, the situation is complicated by the possibility—mainly suggested by the circumstances of Bg (see below)—that the *Commemoratio Brevis* is made up of two originally separate treatises, the one (α) concerned with the psalm tones, and the other (β) concerned with more general matters of performance practice. Since this conjecture does not affect most of the relationships—only three sources include the latter portion—it has been assumed in the following *stemma*. It is impossible, of course, to tell whether the fragments derive from a source which combined the two parts, but the circumstances of Bg might suggest that they did not. α' represents a version which contained both additions and defects. γ is the source of readings common to both sets of fragments. It has seemed necessary to postulate the existence of defective sources δ and ε because there are a few variants which set the two groups of fragments apart, and because a single source for them would be difficult to reconcile with the differing length of the text of each group. W and P would seem to stem from a source ζ which already combined the α and β treatises. It should be kept in mind that there were certainly more stages than are here represented. It seems quite certain that P was copied directly from W, and P2 from P1.

Table 1

A Diagram Showing the Probable Relationship of the Sources

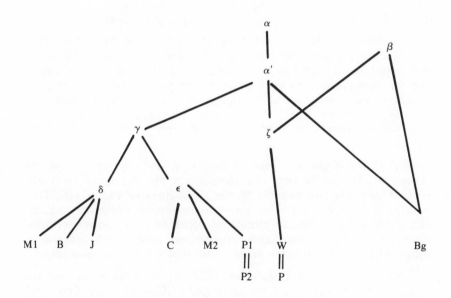

Double lines indicate a direct relationship.
Greek letters stand for lost or conjectural sources.

THE CONTENTS AND STRUCTURE OF THE TREATISE

The arrangement of the *Commemoratio Brevis* is as follows:

I — introduction (the necessity for correct psalmody) (2-8)
II — nomenclature and relationships of the eight modes (9-15)
III — the eight echematic formulas and the eight psalm-tones for the Gospel Canticles (16-36)
IV — the eight tones for the psalter antiphons (37-46)
V — special tones (47-51)
VI — terminations and medians for the first and second tones (52-71)
VII — additional medians for the first and second tones (72-78)
VIII — terminations and medians for the remaining tones (79-98)
IX — concerning modal ambiguity (99-6)
X — concerning spurious psalm-tones *(7)*
XI — concerning regularity of singing *(8-17)*
XII — concerning the pitch of the singing *(18-23)*
XIII — concerning the speed of singing *(23-29)*
XIV — conclusion (differing practices for the psalms; the necessity for rhythmic regularity and its early teaching) *(30-34)*.

The treatise, as it stands, is not a completely unified document, nor has it reached us exactly as it was conceived. The following observations may suggest some of the stages in its evolution.

Section III stands apart from the treatise in three respects: (1) it employs a different and older notation,[10] (2) the psalm tones and antiphons it contains differ in some details from those found later in the treatise, and (3) it presents complete psalm-tones instead of adopting the methodical treatment of *initia, medietates* and *differentiae*. It seems likely that the compiler of the *Commemoratio Brevis* incorporated a chart which had been in use for teaching purposes.

That the *Commemoratio Brevis* is a compilation is demonstrated further in Section IV. Here again are the eight complete psalm-tones, set successively to the eight lines of Psalm 118. This portion of the treatise (39-46) forms a convenient mnemonic which, like Section III, probably circulated separately. It too ignores the problems of the medians and terminations, and it too presents a usage which differs in some details from that set out subsequently.

Section VII is evidently an addition: it contains mostly redundant examples, examples arranged differently—in first and second mode alternately—than elsewhere in the treatise; and it employs a different terminology (*Dorius* for *protus*) for the modes.

---

[10]   See below, p. 19.

The inclusion in Section VIII of the eighth-tone terminations (96) is unexpected, for remarks made earlier in the treatise (80) would seem to have made them unnecessary. These terminations are a later addition to the *Commemoratio,* probably made to repair the early loss of the second-tone *differentiae,* which originally were meant to serve the eighth tone as well.

Section X, a brief remark about spurious psalm-tones, is probably an addition, or at least out of place. It follows as a curious *non sequitur* the preceding comments on tonal ambiguity (Section IX) and would more understandably find place earlier in the treatise.

The concluding portion of the *Commemoratio* (sections IX-XIV) could, with respect to its content, form a separate treatise on the performance practice of Gregorian Chant, and probably originated as a separate document. It is found in the Bamberg manuscript in an earlier position than the fragment of the *Commemoratio* concerned with the psalm tones, and it is found there under its own rubric *(De Laudis Dei Disciplina Sermo).* It should also be noted, in this regard, that the remarks at the close of Section VIII (97-98) are in the nature of a conclusion, and may formerly have served to end the treatise.

Something must be said here about the chart of the *echemata* which follows the *Commemoratio Brevis* in both the Wolfenbüttel and St.-Paul manuscripts, and which Gerbert included as part of the treatise. The evidence which led Gerbert to do so was adventitious: the chart and the *Commemoratio* are found together as the only contents of the St.-Paul manuscript, his source for the *Scriptores* edition. But this circumstance is entirely without weight. While the manuscript in modern times may have circulated "à part, comme manuel indépendant," [11] an older foliation visible at the top, centre, in the manuscript reveals that it was formerly a part of a larger book (doubtless, like the Wolfenbüttel manuscript from which it was copied, a compendium of theoretical treatises).

Other considerations lead to the conclusion that the chart had nothing to do with the *Commemoratio.* For one thing it has absolutely no reference to the treatise: it contains quite different versions of the echematic formulas, and it uses the Byzantine order (which Gerbert arbitrarily changed in his edition) for the modes, arranging them in two groups, the four authentic and the four plagal. The chart is found independent of the *Commemoratio Brevis* in Paris, Bibl. Nat. lat. 7202 [12] (f. 56v). It is reproduced in Appendix III.

---

[11] HUGLO, *Les tonaires,* 63.
[12] Not 7212 as given by Coussemaker (*Mémoire,* 104).

LOSSES AND DISORDERINGS

The *Commemoratio Brevis* has suffered a number of losses, the most important being:

1) the antiphon cue for Ex. 12

2) the syllables for the eighth-mode echematic formula in Ex. 15

3) all of the terminations for Tone 2 (Ex. 39) and one for Tone 8 (Ex. 67)

4) (seemingly) a number of the "manners" of singing the medians of the first four tones.

This last item requires some comment. The arrangement of the examples of medians in the treatise is confused: some would appear to be missing, others, although given under a single rubric, are not metrically similar. Some of this confusion may be owing to copyists' errors, but there is some reason to think that the presentation of the examples in the treatise may never have been thoroughly thought out. Consider the case of the first tone. The *Commemoratio* was evidently set up to display six adaptations of the mediant melody to accommodate the varying number of syllables in a Latin cadence of two accents. There are, in theory, six "normal"[13] variations, namely:

1) $'\!- \, '\!-$
2) $'\!- - \, '\!-$ $\cdot\cdot$
3) $'\!- - \, '\!- -$
4) $'\!- \, '\!- -$
5) $'\!- - \, '$
6) $'\!- \, '$

but in practice a final accented syllable (usually a monosyllable) is always treated as unaccented: the fifth pattern above being accommodated by the first, and number 6 as the second member of either the third or fourth pattern. In fact, only the first four of the above variations need ever concern a singer, and it is these alone which the *Commemoratio* includes (*Modus Quintus* and *Sextus* are left empty). The situation is similar for the second and fourth psalm-tones: the format of the treatise provides for six "manners" but fewer actually appear. It is not therefore surprising to find that the third tone has "lost" some of its medians, or that after the fourth tone the treatise abandons this "systematic" presentation altogether.

---

[13] The rare situations in which text accents are separated by three or more unstressed syllables are not treated systematically in the treatise.

THE HISTORICAL POSITION OF THE
COMMEMORATIO BREVIS

For the purposes of the present discussion, as later when the matter of the importance of the treatise is considered, it is necessary to treat the *Commemoratio Brevis* separately as a document of *musica theorica* and *musica practica*.

Whatever the general validity of the term "dark ages" it has a special and precise meaning for the history of the theory of music. Between Cassiodorus in the sixth century and the Frankish scholars of the ninth no writer seems to have attempted a systematic treatment of musical theory or practice, certainly no treatise survives from this long period to shed light on the development of the music of the western Church, a music whose monuments rank with the great cathedrals and the best of the artistic and spiritual heritage of the post-classical European civilization. With the intellectual re-awakening of the Carolingian Renaissance this period of obscurity came to a close.

But the new *musica theorica* is more than a continuation of the doctrines of classical antiquity. There is, of course, no question that the ideas of the ancient Greeks, especially through the medium of the works of Boethius and Martianus Capella, were taken by the medieval scholars as the principal basis of their writings. But there are also in evidence what are presumably more modern, "eastern" elements: certain concepts and terminology which found their way to the West through Frankish contacts with the Byzantine Empire and Church. The ultimate source of these eastern elements is not as easy to document as the classical component in medieval music theory, but the reason for their inclusion is clear enough: they were necessary to supply the deficiencies of classic theory and terminology in dealing with music which had a substantial near-eastern component. The *Commemoratio Brevis,* no less than the other Frankish writings on music, displays this duality of tradition.

To the eastern tradition belong the concept of four paired-modes and their terminology: protos, deuteros, tritus, tetrardus; autentus, plagis. The Byzantine origin of these terms is made clear from references such as the following, which dates from before 850 A.D.: "Nomina autem eorum apud nos usitata *ex auctoritate Grecorum.*"[14] Similarly to the East belong the mysterious intonation syllables *noanoeane, noeais, anne,* and so on, for it was to a visitor from the Byzantine Empire that Aurelian of Réomé turned for their explanation.[15] These syllables, recent in the West, were of long stand-

---

[14]   HUGLO, *Les tonaires,* 50.
[15]   GS I, 42.

ing in the Eastern Church, although perhaps not indigenous, for even as early as the middle of the ninth century Aurelian's informant was at a loss to explain them.[16] To the musical theory of Greek antiquity belong the analysis of the gamut as a series of tetrachords, the reference to the Dorian mode (*melo Dorio*, probably a later addition, see above, p. 6) and—ultimately—the basic principle of the daseian notation.[17]

The *Commemoratio Brevis* forms part of a clearly definable corpus of early speculative writings on music, whose constitution and customary order in the manuscript tradition is given below:[18]

the *De Institutione Musica* of Boethius
the *Musica Enchiriadis* and its *Scholia*
the *Commemoratio Brevis*
Super unum concavum lignum
Ecce modorum sive tonorum
Hucbald's *Musica*
Divisio monochordi in diatonico genere
the *Alia Musica.*

Although it is numbered among the earliest of the medieval writings on music the *Commemoratio Brevis* is not a seminal document in the history of musical theory. Its importance in this respect is greatly overshadowed by the information it contains on practical matters. It is indebted for its theoretical principles and vocabulary to earlier writings, chiefly:

a)   a very old text, perhaps even from the eighth century, giving the Byzantine nomenclature for the modes. Michel Huglo has traced the descent of this passage, which he believes to have originated in a tonary, to its incorporation in Chapter VIII of Aurelian's *Musica Disciplina.*[19]

b)   Hucbald's *Musica*

c)   the *Musica Enchiriadis* and its *Scholia.*

This leaves very little unaccounted for, although a few details are worth mentioning, namely the reminiscences of St Augustine's *De Musica* III, 1 *(14)* ; St Benedict's *Regula,* chapters XVI (2) and XIX

---

[16]   For a discussion of the meaning of the echematic syllables see T. BAILEY, *The Intonation Formulas of Western Chant* (Toronto, 1974), 20-26.

[17]   See CHARTIER, *La "Musica."*

[18]   This reconstitution was made by Yves Chartier (*op. cit.*) after studying more than twenty-five manuscripts of the *Musica Enchiriadis,* HUCBALD's *Musica* and the *Alia Musica.*

[19]   HUGLO, *Les tonaires*, 47 ff. To the texts gathered by Huglo one should add that of Oxford, MS Bodl. Canon. misc. 212, f. 39v-40.

(4); and the Biblical book of Wisdom, XI, 21 *(10)*. The neo-classical term *melo Dorio* (72) is doubtless owing to the influence of the *Alia Musica*.

While the *Commemoratio Brevis* has affinities with a number of earlier writings, there is a direct source for most of its ideas. Within the corpus of theoretical texts enumerated above there is an evident dependency upon the *Musica Enchiriadis* and its *Scholia*. First, there is the matter of the musical notation: the *Commemoratio*, the *Enchiriadis* and the *Scholia* employ the same daseian signs, and all three make use, for some of their examples, of the same modification of the diastematic-syllabic notation introduced by Hucbald.[20] The *Commemoratio* and the two *Enchiriadis* treatises use the same (or nearly the same[21]) musical terminology. And there are a number of striking textual parallels, the most important of which are set out below in Table 2.

Table 2

TEXTUAL PARALLELS BETWEEN THE COMMEMORATIO BREVIS AND THE ENCHIRIADIS TREATISES

Quos ad euidentiorem intellectum aut sonorum signis aut per sonorum uelut cordas singvlas subtus annotare curaui. (18)	...exempla: quae dupliciter ad evidentiorem intellectum describere conatus sum, et linealiter quidem veluti chordarum usu, et singulatim notarum appositione per syllabas. (ME, GS I, 157) Sic ut prius ex sonorum signis... (ME, GS I, 164)
Assvmatur itaque primi toni neuma regvlaris... (19)	Exempli gratia, usitata neuma regularis ad primum tonum... (SE, GS I, 179)
Noeane [etc.] non sunt uerba aliquid significantia sed syllabae ad inuestigandam melodiam aptae. (38)	Ad hunc modum consuetis utuntur modulis ad investigandam toni... utpote *Noannoeane* et *Noeagis* et caetera, quae putamus non tam significativa esse verba, quam syllabas modulationi attributas. (ME, GS I, 158)
(Cf. Commemoratio, *12-17*)	Quatenus uti quae syllabae breves, quae sunt longae, attenditur... ut ea, quae diu, ad ea, quae non diu, legitime concurrant. (ME, GS I, 182. Cf. St AUGUSTINE, *De Musica* III, 1.) Sic itaque numerose est canere, longis brevibusque sonis ratas morulas metiri, nec per loca protrahere magis quam

---

[20] CHARTIER, *La "Musica,"* Introduction.
[21] See below p. 12.

oportet, sed infra scandendi legem
vocem continere, ut possit melum ea
finiri mora, qua cepit. Verum si aliquo-
tiens causa variationis mutare moram
velis, id est circa initium aut finem pro-
tensiorem vel incitatiorem cursum
facere, duplo id feceris, id est ut pro-
ductam moram in duplo correptiore seu
correptam immutes, duplo longiore.
(ME, GS I, 183)

...in alteram transeat et in nouam   ...at in octavis in novam mutetur.
mutetvr. *(20)*   (ME, GS I, 163)

Although the association of the *Commemoratio Brevis* and the two *Enchiriadis* treatises is close, they are certainly not by the same author, nor from the same monastery: there are a few differences in the musical terminology ("terminales" [22], for example, in place of the "finales" of the *Musica Enchiriadis,*[22] and the different use of "sonus"[23]); and the treatises include quite different versions of the echematic formulas.[24]

So far this discussion has centred on the *Commemoratio Brevis* as a theoretical treatise. As a document of the medieval *musica practica* the treatise stands in quite a different relationship to the history of music. Considered from a certain aspect the work might be counted among the abbreviated "teaching" tonaries; it certainly owes something of its content and organization to earlier Frankish books of this type.[25] But the *Commemoratio Brevis* is only incidentally a tonary. It is principally a treatise on psalmody, and in this respect it stands at the very beginning of the written tradition. Its sources, if we here consider the two mnemonic charts mentioned above on page 6 to have been incorporated, are—as far as is known —purely oral teachings. It is important to note, however, that the author has looked afield for this information (*prout potui de diversis collecta* [30]). The oral teachings doubtless derive from more than one locality.

Tonaries subsequent to the *Commemoratio Brevis* normally supply an illustrative psalm-tone for each of the eight modes. Michel Huglo has suggested that this practice might be owing to the influence of our treatise.[26] Beyond this, the direct influence of the *Commemoratio Brevis,* that is to say its historical position with

---

[22] GS I, 152.
[23] See the entry in the Glossary.
[24] Concerning the local diversity of these formulas see BAILEY, *The Intonation Formulas,* 36-39.
[25] HUGLO, *Les tonaires,* 29.
[26] *Ibid.,* 65.

respect to later psalmodic practice, is hard to document. It is clear that the author of the *Commemoratio Brevis,* or perhaps it would be better here to call him the compiler, had it in mind to create a *vade mecum* of universal application, for both the monastic and secular establishments.[27] The treatise seems not to have been very widely distributed. But it inaugurated a continuing process, the reduction to order of the diverse and diffuse oral traditions for the psalms, a process which, as has already been mentioned, was fairly complete for the main features of the psalmody by the twelfth or thirteenth century,[28] but which cannot be said to have been concluded until the issuance of the uniform Vatican Edition in the twentieth century.

THE DATE AND PROVENANCE

The date of the *Commemoratio Brevis* cannot be determined with any certainty. There is an obviously close relationship with the *Musica Enchiriadis,* which recent musical scholarship places in the last decade of the ninth century.[29] The most likely conjecture for the *Commemoratio Brevis* is that it was written shortly afterward, around the beginning of the tenth century. There seems to be little probability that the *Enchiriadis* was antedated by the *Commemoratio.* It is hardly conceivable that a brief practical manual could be the source of such a systematic theoretical treatise. Besides, there are other indications. The *Musica Enchiriadis* is evidently introducing the daseian notation, explaining it as a novelty.[30] The *Commemoratio Brevis* employs the symbols without explanation. This same consideration applies to the second of the incorporated mnemonic charts (see above, page 6); it too must date from after the composition of the *Musica Enchiriadis* in about 895 A.D. The first chart may be a little older, although not much, for it employs the diastematic-syllabic notation introduced by Hucbald in his *Musica,* written about 885.[31] It is not probable that the *Commemoratio Brevis* was written after any great interval, for the manuscript tradition goes back to the tenth century, and the daseian notation was soon rendered obsolete by diastematic neumes, which make their appearance as early as c. 935 in Aquitanian service-books.[32]

---

[27] In mentioning the number of psalms at Vespers the *Commemoratio* refers to both the monastic and canonial usage *(22)*.

[28] See G. REESE, *Music in the Middle Ages* (New York, 1940), 173.

[29] HUGLO, *Les tonaires*, 61.

[30] GS I, 152-153.

[31] CHARTIER, *La "Musica,"* Introduction.

[32] Paris, Bibl. Nat. lat. 1240.

The provenance of the *Commemoratio Brevis* is also elusive. The thirty-eight antiphons cited in the treatise were nearly all in general use,[33] and the two or three exceptions provide no apparent consensus, even if such scant evidence could be considered convincing. It goes without saying that local details of the early psalmodic practice are too little known to allow the demonstration of any affinities by this kind of comparison.[34] The appearance in the treatise of an unusual sign, viz ~ (its interpretation is discussed below), does not, unfortunately, provide the clear indication one might hope for. This sign, as a symbol for the quilisma, has been noted as a characteristic of Chartres and Laon.[35] However it is also a feature of the Celebrated Montpellier Codex,[36] whose origin may be the Northwest of France, perhaps Normandy[37]—or Dijon.[38] This is not very conclusive, but what remains, a possible attribution to the northern half of France, seems to be supported by the evidence of a few variants in the psalm texts.[39]

In the absence of hard facts only inference can take us further. Since daseian signs had an extremely limited diffusion, it is reasonable to suppose that the region in which they were introduced also gave rise to the *Commemoratio Brevis*. Once again the argument turns on the association with the *Musica Enchiriadis*. This treatise, on the basis of the most recent research, is thought to have been written between the Seine and Rhine rivers in northern France,[40] probably in the region of Saint-Amand. The best conjecture for the *Commemoratio Brevis* is that it was written in a Benedictine monastery[41] in the same general area.

---

[33] That is to say, they are found in most of the manuscripts of René-Jean HESBERT's *Corpus Antiphonalium Officii* (Rome, 1963-70).

[34] Huglo has suggested (*Les tonaires*, 63) a special affinity with Einsiedeln, because "les quatre différences psalmodiques du premier ton ... sont identiques" in the *Commemoratio* and Einsiedeln MS 79. The fact is, they are not identical, nor is there in the case of the other tones any particular similarity. Ferretti has also (*Esthétique*, 305), on the very slightest evidence, implied a relationship between the *Commemoratio* and Einsiedeln.

[35] *Paléographie musicale*, XI, 108, 115.

[36] *Paléographie musicale*, VII, 18.

[37] WAESBERGHE, *The Theory*, I, 86.

[38] *La notation musicale des chants liturgiques latins* (ed. by the Monks of Solesmes, 1960). See the commentary to Example 43.

[39] HUGLO, *Les tonaires*, 64, note 3.

[40] *Ibid.*, 61.

[41] "Debitum servitutis nostrae" (2) and "corde quam qui voce" (4) are phrases from the Rule (*Regula S. Benedicti*, XVI, XIX). "Opus Dei" (3) is a Benedictine designation.

THE TESTIMONY OF THE TREATISE

Although the *Commemoratio Brevis* is not of great interest to the history of musical theory in general, its evidence does bear on one or two related matters. The treatise contains one of the very earliest appearances of the western intonation formulas adapted from the Byzantine *echemata,* and the characteristic melismas which originated in the West.[42] (The chart included by Gerbert as part of the *Commemoratio,* and given in this edition in the Appendix, presents another version of these formulas.) The appearance of the intonation formulas in the *Commemoratio Brevis* is exceedingly valuable, since they are written in daseian symbols, a musical notation which is absolutely pitch-accurate.

The treatise also contains something of importance on the matter of ambiguities of modal classification. It is the first work which takes up the problem of antiphons of the type *Benedicta tu* and *Ex Egypto,* assigning them to the second mode and specifying an irregular psalm-tone. Earlier tonaries assign such antiphons to the fourth mode.[43] The *Commemoratio* also has something of interest to say about the criteria for deciding the tonality. Earlier theorists, Aurelian of Réomé and Regino of Prüm, for example, make it quite clear that in antiphonal chants it is the beginning which determines the mode.[44] The *Commemoratio Brevis* is the first treatise to put forward the modern approach maintained by Guido of Arezzo, John Cotton and all later writers, that it is the end of the chant which decides the matter.

But the greatest importance of the *Commemoratio Brevis* lies in the information it contains on practical music making. This may be subsumed under two headings.

a) THE PSALMODIC PRACTICE

The author of the *Commemoratio* does not claim to have reconciled all local practices ("non preiudicans illis qui easdem modulationes licet aliter" [*30*]) nor has he been completely successful in reducing psalmody to an order based on clear principles. The practice for the psalms set out by the treatise is not, by any means, completely systematic. First of all, certain questions of detail are ap-

---

[42] See BAILEY, *The Intonation Formulas,* 11-15.

[43] HUGLO, *Les tonaires,* 64. Huglo has unfortunately mistaken the opening of the appended melisma for the psalm tone. Readers of his book would therefore suppose that the *Commemoratio* assigned the regular second-mode psalm tone to such antiphons.

[44] W. APEL, *Gregorian Chant* (Bloomington, 1958), 174.

parently left open. Compare, for example, the setting of "suam" and "eius" in the termination of the psalm tone given in Example 26, or the text setting of the *initium* of the regular seventh tone in Example 23 and Example 66 ("Confitebor," "Benedictus," "Et erexit"). More importantly, the *Commemoratio,* while it teaches a method for adapting the eight regular psalm-tones ostensibly to any antiphon, includes a good number of special tones—the remnants, evidently, of an earlier practice—for certain antiphons whose attribution to any of the eight modes was problematical, or whose association with an exceptional tone was established. In this respect the treatise may be seen to represent an intermediate stage between early, unsettled and diffuse practices and the later standard system it helped formulate. Perhaps the most important systematic discrepancy of the treatise is the unresolved application of two opposite principles with respect to the text, the cursive and the accentual. According to the first— doubtless the earlier[45]—the psalms are sung to the melodies without regard for the text-accent; according to the other, the configuration of the psalm-melodies is altered to reinforce the textual accent. (These two opposing principles were never resolved entirely; both play a part in the final codification of the psalmody in the books of Soles- mes.) In the treatise the *initia* are all cursive. The median cadences are mostly accentual, of two accents, but some one-accent cadences also occur, and some which are purely cursive. The second-*initia* (after the caesura) are sometimes accentual[46] and sometimes cursive, as are the terminations *(differentiae).* This is not the place to enter into a discussion of the differences between the psalmody of the *Commemoratio Brevis* and the later standard practice represented by the Solesmes books, but the following features of the ancient usage should be noted:

1) the *initia* were normally repeated for all verses of the psalm,

2) the canticle tones used the simple *initia,*

3) the second-*initia* were not restricted to ornate psalmody,

4) there is no trace of a flex; very long verses are divided with two median cadences,

5) the reciting-note for the third tone was *b,*

6) the antiphon was repeated after each psalm verse.

b) GENERAL PERFORMANCE PRACTICES

The point of departure in the reconstruction of a musical per- formance practice is the notation, or more specifically, the failings

---

[45]   See T. BAILEY, "Accentual and Cursive Cadences in Gregorian Psalmody," in *Journal of the American Musicological* Society, xxix/3 (Fall, 1976).

[46]   Cf. Ex. 50, "et synagoga," "opprobrium hominum."

of the notation. No method has ever been devised—unless we consider sound recording to be included—that will express completely the intentions of the composer. Much of the information not included in any notation we care to take as an example was at one time generally known, and with respect to the period in which the music was written, quite unnecessary to specify. But this unspecified information is forgotten by subsequent generations, the amount forgotten bearing a direct relationship to the number of years which intercede. So it is in the case of Gregorian Chant, whose best documents were written at a distance of a thousand years and at a time when musical notation was at a very primitive stage. Our uncertainty is not confined to matters of nuance or detail, but extends to fundamental questions of correct pitches and rhythms.

The recovery of the correct pitches of the chants has been very largely successful, through the methods of scientific text criticism initiated by the scholars of Solesmes. In this recovery sources like the *Commemoratio Brevis* and the celebrated Montpellier Codex, which give the chants in symbols whose exact pitch equivalent is known, are of very great value, for they are the Rosetta Stones which make possible the decipherment of the early cheironomic manuscripts, whose notation is very defective in this respect. The recovery of the rhythm of the Chant is very much more difficult, and no general agreement has been reached even though controversy has been carried on for the better part of a century. There is nothing to be gained by repeating here the arguments for this or that interpretation of the evidence. In short, there are two basic positions, that of the "equalists"[48] who maintain that all notes of the chant are of more or less equal duration—notwithstanding slight differences in expressive nuance—and that of the "mensuralists"[49] who hold that the notes of chants have different durations with a fixed proportional relationship. Most scholars who are not partisan would conclude that there is some historical authority for both positions, that in the earliest centuries the chant was sung proportionally, but in the later Middle Ages this practice was abandoned in favour of the smooth, so-called oratorical rhythm of the "plainchant."

The evidence of the *Commemoratio Brevis*, especially *8-16* and *31-33* in the text, is one of the most important buttresses of the mensuralist position. As Gregory Murray remarked, "Its obvious im-

---

[47] *Paléographie musicale* vol. VII-VIII.

[48] The chief exponent is André Mocquereau. See his *Nombre musical grégorien* (Tournai, 1908).

[49] The evidence for the accentual interpretation is set out by Gregory MURRAY in his *Gregorian Rhythm in the Gregorian Centuries* (Bath, 1957). See also J.W.A. VOLLAERTS, *Rhythmic Proportions in Early Medieval Ecclesiastical Chant* (Leiden, 1958).

portance is matched by its luminous clarity." [50] The "luminous clarity" of the testimony has nevertheless not prevented André Mocquereau from citing those portions which emphasized the necessity for "evenness" in singing in support of the Solesmes equalist point of view. Mocquereau simply dismissed the rest out of hand: [51]

> Le reste du texte est altéré, le sens général qui s'en dégage n'est pas nécessaire à notre dessein, et la première partie en est si claire, si précise, qu'elle n'a besoin d'aucune explication.

The passage referred to was obviously defective in the Gerbert edition, the source for the text of the *Commemoratio* studied by Mocquereau. It is interesting to wonder whether he would have accorded the treatise more authority had he been acquainted with the readings of the Wolfenbüttel and Bamberg manuscripts.

In addition to its evidence on the rhythm of the Chant, the *Commemoratio* sets out the general considerations which governed the speed of the singing *(23-29)* and the level at which it was pitched *(18-23)*. But no less valuable are the insights which are given incidentally. The reference to female secular singers *(cantrices seculares* [6]), evidently of a professional calibre, is particularly interesting, as is the clear indication that the Chant was to be judged on aesthetic grounds, prized as an art as well as for its spiritual significance *(2-7)*.

THE NOTATION

The *Commemoratio Brevis* employs two notational systems. The one used most extensively thoughout the treatise is the daseian notation of the *Musica Enchiriadis*. [52] The pitch equivalents of its symbols are indicated below:

Table 3

THE DASEIAN NOTATION

| Graves | Terminales | Superiores | Excellentes |

---

[50]   *Gregorian Rhythm*, 14.
[51]   *Le nombre*, I, 19.
[52]   For a discussion of the evolution of the daseian notation see CHARTIER, *La "Musica."*

The four disjunct tetrachords *(graves, terminales, superiores, excellentes)* are symmetrical, each with the intervals, tone-semitone-tone, the resulting scale featuring augmented octaves. Although the notation is explicit, there must remain some doubt whether *b-flat* and *f'-natural* were not possibilities.[53]

The *Commemoratio* augments the daseian symbols of the *Musica Enchiriadis* with three signs. The first of these, the dot, used to articulate the melismas in Example 1, 3, 5, 7, *etc.*, was intended to indicate the groupings of neumatic notation. The manuscripts seem to be quite careless about these dots (perhaps their meaning was not understood by later copyists); even the best sources seem to have lost some. The second sign, viz ⌐ , is more problematical. In its ascending position it evidently signifies a quilisma. This can be readily affirmed by comparing the melodies in the treatise with neumatic versions in other manuscripts. In its descending position its interpretation is uncertain.[54] This sign was evidently meaningless to some of the scribes, for it is confused very often with the articulation dots mentioned above. The third additional sign is a horizontal line, used only in the second mnemonic chart (39-46), which serves (unnecessarily) to indicate the repetition of a pitch for successive syllables:

ᵧᶠ—————— ᵧᶠ ᶈᵖ
mandasti mandata.

Examples 2-16 of the treatise employ the diastematic-syllabic notation introduced by Hucbald,[55] but with a slight modification. In addition to the interlinear indications T (tone) and S (semi-tone) the *Commemoratio*, as did the *Musica Enchiriadis*, indicates by means of adjacent daseian symbols the exact pitch of each syllable.

THE PRINCIPLES OF THE EDITION

The main source for the present edition is the Wolfenbüttel manuscript (W). Supplementary readings have been incorporated from other manuscripts where W is incomplete or where another reading is more correct, thus *placeat* is given in place of *placet* (5) and *subtus* in place of the bizarre *sumptus* (18). All variant spellings have been noted in the critical apparatus. The only exception is the distinction between *u* and *v*; in this respect the edition follows the

---

[53] See REESE, *Music in the Middle Ages*, 254.
[54] *Paléographie musicale* VII, 18.
[55] See note 31.

Wolfenbüttel manuscript. Capitals have been supplied here and there, for all proper names, and for *Dominus* and *Deus*. In the case of proper names there has been no attempt to regularize the spellings, thus, for example, *Israel* and *Israhel* both appear. The medieval *e* in place of the classical diphthong *ae* has been corrected only where there is a consensus for the older spelling in the manuscripts. All contractions have been expanded without comment. Punctuation has been supplied, although in almost every case it follows that of the manuscripts.

Since Gerbert's sources are certainly included among those of the present edition, his redaction published in *Scriptores Ecclesiastici de Musica Sacra Potissimum* (1784) I, 213-228 has not been collated. Gerbert's readings, keeping in mind his habit of making minor corrections independent of the authentic text, can all be traced to the St.-Paul manuscript (P). His editorial contributions included standardizing the spelling and supplying, here and there, a subjunctive; but it included also the omission of some words and the mistaking or miscopying of some of the daseian signs. The present edition is more complete than Gerbert's in two places: for the discussion of the relative duration of breves and longs *(12)*, and at the conclusion of the treatise *(33-34)*.

The critical apparatus is as concise as possible. The text has been numbered by sentences in two consecutive series: 1-99 and *1-34*; in this way it was possible to avoid a very great number of footnote references. Unless it is specifically noted, the readings of the manuscripts are the same as those of the edition. This applies, in the case of the musical examples, to any syllables given without daseian signs (the critical apparatus contains no partial words). When a variant is only a matter of spelling or word order the reading from the text is usually not repeated below. For those cases where a word appears more than once in a sentence, the adjacent word is given in parentheses to identify which appearance is at issue in the apparatus. This sign ' in the Latin text indicates the beginning of a new page.

The present writer is quite aware of the difficulties of translating a work like the *Commemoratio Brevis*. Many scholars have concluded that such attempts are ultimately futile. The fact is, however, that there are many who will wish to read the treatise who do not know Latin. While the translation may be bound to contain misrepresentations, the authentic text is given here between the same covers, and it is hoped that even those who would understand only a few words will wish to consult it on some points. The interpretation of a number of terms—these are all included in the Glossary—has been based more on musical than philological considerations. Some words, although their translation might seem obvious, present unexpected difficulties. In the case of *tonus*, for example, it was decided to keep with the long-established English usage, translating the word as "mode" even though for many reasons "tone" might have been preferred.[56] As for the general character of the translation, the fact that it is published with the Latin has provided the freedom to be a little less literal, and perhaps a little more literary.

Short passages from the *Commemoratio Brevis* have been cited and translated by many authors contributing to the seemingly endless controversy over the rhythmic interpretation of the Chant. Coussemaker, in his *Mémoire sur Hucbald,* claimed to be including a translation and transcription of the entire treatise.[57] Coussemaker's work was based, as we have already noted, on a faulty version of the *Commemoratio,* but more than that, it is careless and frequently incorrect. Many passages—including, one suspects, any which caused difficulty—are silently omitted.

The musical examples printed with the translation have been transcribed from daseia into modern staff-notation. Since the use of standard notation would imply rhythms not indicated by the daseian signs, note-heads alone have been employed, with phrasing marks to indicate groups of notes to be sung to a single syllable, or in the case of melismas, to indicate the articulation of the dots in the manuscripts. It was mentioned earlier that these dots have been treated casually by the copyists. This edition contains only those found in the Wolfenbüttel manuscript. The appearances or omission of the dots in the other sources have not been collated. A jagged mark (w) in place of a note-head indicates a quilisma. A note-head with a stroke (x) is used for the sign ∼ , whose significance in the descending position is uncertain. A double bar is used following a final cadence, whether of a psalm verse or antiphon; a single bar-line follows the median cadence at the caesura. The beginning of the second or third member of each psalm-verse is marked with an asterisk. The texts of the musical examples have not, of course, been translated; they are given exactly as in the Latin version of the treatise.

Many of the antiphon cues are given without daseian signs. It seemed best not to supply them for the Latin text. For the translation, however, the cues have been completed, whenever possible from the nearly contemporary Hartker Antiphoner.[58]

The psalms of the *Commemoratio Brevis* are those of the Gallican Psalter, which was adopted for the Roman Liturgy at the close of the eighth century. But it will be immediately obvious that the

---

[56] Chartier has assembled the texts which relate to the medieval controversy over the use of *modus* and *tonus* (*La "Musica,"* Commentary).

[57] Pp. 89-104.

[58] *Paléographie musicale,* series 2, vol. I.

verses of the treatise are in many cases at variance with the standard versions, not only in details of wording, but even with respect to the place chosen to divide the psalm verse or end it. Some of the variants are, as Huglo has noticed,[59] owing to contamination by the older *Romanum* translation of the psalms, which survived in a great many of the ancient chants of the Mass and Office. But many of the variants cannot be understood in this way. The simplest explanation is that the compiler of the *Commemoratio Brevis* was relying on his memory, and in these instances his recollection was not letter-perfect. There was no point in correcting the psalms in the treatise, and since it may be supposed that everyone has access to a Latin Bible, it was thought unnecessary to provide the corrected readings. The psalm verses which are at variance with the standard Vulgate versions are all indicated in the List of Psalms, page 116.

---

[59]   *Les tonaires*, 64, note 3.

CONSPECTUS ABBREVIATIONUM

A. CODICUM ET LIBRORUM IMPRESSORUM ABBREVIATIONES

Ba Barcelona Arc. Cor. Arag. Rip 42 (ff. 57v-58)
Bg Bamberg Var. 1 (ff. 38v-40v, 42v-46v)
C   Cambridge Corpus Christi 260 (ff. 51v-53v)
J   Cracow Jagel. 1965 (pp. 59-60)
M1 Munich Clm 14649 (ff. 32v-33)
M2 Munich Clm 14272 (ff. 173v-174)
P   St.-Paul (Kärnten) 29.4.2 (132/6) (ff. 1-9)
P1 Paris Bibl. Nat. lat. 7212 (ff. 36-37v)
P2 Paris Bibl. Nat. lat. 7211 (ff. 49-51)
W   Wolfenbüttel 4376 (ff. 82v-87)
GS GERBERT, *Scriptores Ecclesiastici de Musica Sacra Potissimum*

B. ABBREVIATIONES ET SIGNA QUAE ADHIBENTUR IN APPARATU CRITICO

A :   antiphona
add :   addit, addunt
al man : alia manu recentiori
cor :   correxit
c n :   cum notis musicis
del :   deleta, deletum
Ex :   exemplum
exp :   explicit
in marg : in margine

men :   mendosa
not :   notatio musica
om :   omisit, omittunt
s n :   sine notis musicis
term :   terminatur, terminantur
< > :   additiones
[ ] :   interpolationes et lacunae
italica : correctiones, emendationes; (in apparatu critico) observationes editoris
* :   secundum vel tertium membrum versuum psalmorum

TEXTUS
and
TRANSLATION

Ba 57v
Bg 42v
C 51v
J 59
M1 32v
M2 173v
P (159)
P1 36
P2 49
W 82v

¹ INCIPIT COMMEMORATIO BREVIS DE TONIS ET PSALMIS MODVLANDIS.

² Debitvm servitvtis nostrae qui ad ministerivm laudationis Domini deputamur, non solum integrum debet esse et plenum, sed decenti quoque conuenientia iucundum atque suaue. ³ Et ideo peritos nos esse conuenit officii nostri ut scienter et ornate confiteamur nomini sancto eius, et gloriemur in carminibus suis, quatinus et Deo nostro' iucunda sit decoraque laudatio, et audientes in operum Dei laudem et reuerentiam exardescant. ⁴ Quamius enim Deo magis placeat qui corde quam qui voce canit, utrumque tamen ex ipso est' et dupliciter prodest si utrvmque fiat, si scilicet et animo apud Deum dulciter canitur, et homines canoris dulcedo sancto affectv commouet.' ⁵ Licet quoque multorum deuotio Deo ualde placeat, qui in psalmodia nec ipsa uerba rite effari queant, nequaquam tamen integrae est ille deuotionis, qui quod exhibere debet, quam optime et quam reuerentissime id possit Deo non exhibet.

P2 49v
Bg 43
C 52

⁶ Citharedae et tibicines et reliqui musicorum uasa ferentes uel etiam cantores et cantrices† seculares omni student conatv quod canitur siue citharizatur ad delec-

P1 36v

---

¹ *Titulus*: DE tonis Et psalmis modulandis J // Ubaldus *al man in marg* W // Otto de tonis *in marg* W
² esse debet Bg // iocundum Ba Bg C J M1 M2 P1 P2
³ quatenus M2 // iocunda Ba Bg C J M1 M2 P1 P2 // laudatio decoraque Ba J M1
⁴ dulce Bg
⁵ deuocio Ba P // placet Ba C M1 M2 P P1 P2 W // affari Ba J M1 P1 P2 // tamen *om* J // integre Ba C P P1 P2 // deuocionis M2 P2 // obtime M2 // possit id J // exibet Ba C // exhibere: exlbet M2
⁶ Citharede P W // Cytharedae Bg M1 // Cytharedi J // Cytharede P1 P2 // mosicorum *cor in* musicorum P2 // cante'tricest† P1 // cantatrices P2 // saeculares C // siue: sine C // cytharizatur Bg J M1 P1 P2

[1] A BRIEF REVIEW OF THE MODES AND OF PSALM SINGING

[2] The service owed by us whose duty it is to perform the Divine Office should be not only full and unstinting but, with proper dignity, agreeable and pleasant. [3] It is fitting therefore that we should be proficient in our duties, so that we may bear witness knowledgeably and gracefully to his holy name and take pride in his chants, so that the worship may be pleasing and beautiful to our Lord, and so that those hearing in the Divine Office things both admirable and reverent may grow ardent. [4] For however much God might prefer the singing of the heart to that of the voice, if they be combined, if the sweet singing of the heart is heard by God and the charm of the voice move men to piety, the effect is doubly pleasing. [5] And even if the devotion of the many who are unable to utter the ritual words in correct psalmody is greatly pleasing to God, by no means satisfactory are the prayers of the man who, being able, does not present them to God as he ought: in the best and most respectful manner.

[6] Players of the cithara, flute and other musical instruments, and secular singers, men and women, all take special care to obey the rules of their art, so that what they sing or play is pleasing to their

tandos audientes artis ratione temperare. ⁷ Nos uero qui meruimus uerba maiestatis in os sumere, nosne sine arte et neglegenter proferimus cantica sanctitatis, ac non magis artis decorem in sacris assvmimus, quo illi abutuntur in nugis?' ⁸ Quapropter paruam hinc noticiam exerciciis vestris ex me destinatam suscipite, ut ex paruorvm scientia fiatis capatiores maiorum. P 1v

⁹ Itaque in octo tonos, quos ita nominamus, melodiam diuidimus, quorum differentias et proprietates ecclesiasticum cantorem, nisi ingenii tarditate obstante, culpabile est ignorare. ¹⁰ E quibus quatvor sunt principales, alii uero' quatvor singvlis principalibus ex latere subiun- P2 50 guntur.' M1 33

¹¹ Primus itaque tonus principalis apud cantores autentus protus, id est auctoralis primus' vocatur. ¹² Cui Bg 43v subiungitur qui plagis protus, id est lateralis uel obliquus primus dicitur. ¹³ Secundus tonus principalis autentus deuteros, id est auc'toralis secundus nominatur,' cum Ba 58 J 60 quo incedit plagis deuteros, id est lateralis secundus. ¹⁴ Tertius principalis autentus tritus, id est auctoralis tertius, et cum eo plagis tritus, hoc est lateralis tertius.' C 52v ¹⁵ Quartus principalis autentus tetrardus, cuius subiugalis est plagis tetrardus, id est lateralis quartvs.

---

⁷ magestatis C // summere J // sumero P1 // nosne sine arte: nonne peccamus si sine arte Ba J M2 // nonne si peccamus sine arte M1 // nosne si arte C P1 P2 // negglegenter *cor in* neglegenter P2 // artem decoram M2 //

⁸ notitiam C M2 P1 P2 // exercitiis Bg J M1 M2 P1 P2 // exerciis C // (vestris) ex: et C // capaciores Bg J M1 P

⁹ diuidiamus C // aeclesiasticum M1 M2 P1 P2 // nisi: non J // obstante <vel culpae> culpabile Bg

¹⁰ Ex (quibus) P // sunt quatuor Ba J M1 P1 P2

¹¹ tonus itaque M1 // principale Ba // auctoralis: auctoris C

¹² cui M2 // lateralis: laterasis P2 // oblicus Ba J P1 P2 // oblicus *cor in* obliqus [*sic*] M2 // primus <vocatur uel> dicitur Bg

¹³ principale Ba // (autentus) deuterus Bg J M1 M2 // incidit Bg // pl[a]gis C // (plagis) deuterus Bg J M1 M2

¹⁴ (secundus) tercius Ba Bg J P2 // (auctoralis) tercius Ba Bg J P P2 // hoc est: id est J // id est *cor in* hoc est M2 // (lateralis) tercius Ba Bg J // lateralis tertius: lateris tereuis P2

¹⁵ plagis *supra* M2 // (autentus) tetrardas C // lateralis: lateris P2

audience. [7] Shall we then who have received the privilege of giving voice to the Divine Praises, shall we sing clumsily and negligently the sacred Chant, and not make greater use of the grace of art for things which are sacred than those who waste it upon trifles? [8] Accept from me therefore this little treatise intended for your instruction: that from a little knowledge you will gain the capacity for more.

[9] Melody is divided into eight modes *(tonos)* [1], as we call them, and to be ignorant of their differences [2] and properties, unless slowness of wit is the impediment, is reprehensible in an ecclesiastical singer. [10] Of these eight modes four are principal; the other four are subordinate, derived from each respectively of the principal modes.

[11] The first principal mode is known to singers as *autentus protus*, that is, "first authentic." [12] Subordinate to this is what is called the *plagis protus*, that is, "first lateral," or "first oblique." [13] The second principal mode is called the *autentus deuteros*, that is, "second authentic," with which is associated the *plagis deuteros*, that is, "second lateral." [14] The third principal is the *autentus tritus*, that is, "third authentic," and its partner is the *plagis tritus*, which is the "third lateral." [15] The fourth principal is *autentus tetrardus*, whose subordinate is the *plagis tetrardus*, that is, the "fourth lateral."

---

[1]   See above, p. 20.
[2]   See the Commentary.

¹⁶ Secundum horum octo tonarum proprietates singulis suis modulationibus ad responsoria nostrates vtvntur, suis item ad maiores antiphonas quae scilicet in introitu ad missas canuntur, siue in fine celebrationis ad communionem. ¹⁷ Porro illos modos per quos psalmi ad antiphonas modulantvr, in hoc opusculo habeo utcumque edicere, reliquis prioribus ob prolixitatem uitatis. ¹⁸ Quos ad euidentiorem intellectum aut sonorum signis aut per sonorum uelut cordas singvlas subtus annotare curaui.

¹⁹ As'sv'matur itaque primi toni neuma regvlaris, W 83 P 2 quae ita se apud nos habet:'

term hic
Ba J M1

[Ex. 1]

No-a-no-e-a-ne

---

¹⁶ [to]norum P W // que M2 P2 // caelebrationis M1 P1 // commun[ion]em Ba
¹⁷ psalmi ad antiphonas modulantur: psalmos et antiphonas modulamur Ba J M1 // psalmos et antiphonas modulantur M2 P1 P2 // antifonas *cor in* antiphonas M2 // hoc *om* M1 // prolixiaem *cor in* prolixitatem M2
¹⁸ chordas C J M1 // singulans C // subtus: sumptus Bg C P P1 P2 W //subter Ba J // adnotare Bg

¹⁹ Asummatur P2 // que P2

Ex. 1: *Neuma imperfecta:* Bg

neuma: C

Nonanoeane M2

neuma: P

Noano-e-ane P1

Noan[o]-e-ane *neuma del* P2

[16] In accordance with the singular properties of these eight modes we employ their respective intonations for the responds and also for the Greater Antiphons such as those sung at the Introit of the Mass or at the end of the service at the Communion. [17] But out of consideration for its length I intend in this little treatise to present only those ways psalms are sung with [Office] antiphons, passing over the other cases mentioned above. [18] That these ways may be more clearly understood I have taken the trouble to notate them below either by pitch-signs or on "strings," each "string," as it were, indicating a pitch.

[19] Following is the standard formula, as it is known to us, for the first mode:

[Ex. 1]

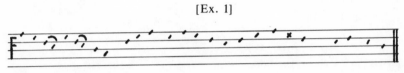

No-a-no-e-a-ne

[20] Sequitur modulatio psalmi quae ascendit usque
devtervm tetracordi superioris in sex consistens sonis:' Bg 44
P2 50v

[Ex. 2]

♂ T	nc					
४ T	a et nu	et se per	n secula seculo			
⋫ T	ri	m	e i		ru	ame
╱ S	Glo		t		m	
℮ T						
⋫						n

P²⁻/P P P⅂ P / P P°
[A] E-   v-ge serue bone'   M2 174

---

[20] que M2 usque <ad> P2 // tetracordi: tetrardi Bg // tetrachordi C P2

Ex. 2: *Not psalmi men* Bg
P ⅃⅃   P ४ ४
et in se-cula seculorum amen C
        ⅃P⅃ ४४ ४ ४ ⅃⅃ ४४ ⅃ P⅃P⅃ PⅤ ४४ ४ ४⅃ ४ ⅃ PⅤ P⅃PⅤ ४ ४ ४`
psalmus: Gloria patri et spi-ri-tui sanc-to si-cut erat et nunc et sem-per et in secula
४ ४ P⅃ P P/PP°
seculorum a-men *al man* M2
P   ⅃⅃   ⅃
et in se-cula amen P1 P2

Euge serue bone *s n* Bg
P P/P P
E- ⅂   uge C
    ⅂ P / PP/PP⅂P P⅂
bone < et fi-de-   lis> M2
P·/P
E-   uge P
P P/P   PP ⅂ P/
E-   uge ser-ue P1 P2

[20] Following is the intonation, which ascends to the second degree of the upper tetrachord and is formed of six scale-steps:

[Ex. 2]

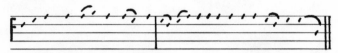

Gloria... et nunc et semper et in secula seculorum amen

⌐A⌐   E-   u-ge serve bone

21 TONUS SECUNDUS SUBIUGALIS PRIMI'

[Ex. 3]

[neume notation]
No-   e-a- is

22 Sequitur modulatio psalmi quae in tetrardum ter-
minalem eleuatur et descendit in tetrardum grauium nixa
sonis quinque:'

[Ex. 4]

		nc et	m					
	e	nu	se	per	e	n secula secu	rv	
		t		r			lo	m
	ria			t i				men
	Glo							a

[neume notation]
[A] Ma-   gnum

---

22   que Bg M2 P2 sonis: sonus P1 // soniis P2
[neume]
Ex. 3: No- eais Bg
om C M2 P1 P2
neuma: *[neume notation]*   P W

Ex. 4: *Not psalmi men* Bg
[neume]
semper e[t] in amen C
[neume notation]
psalmus: Glori-a patri et spi-ri-tu-i sanc-to si-cut secu-lo-rum a-men *al man* M2
[neume]
semper et in amen P1 P2
Magnum *s n* Bg
[neume]
Ma-   gnum C
Magnum *om* M2 P1 P2
[neume]
Ma-   [g]num P
[A] Consurge consurge *add s n in marg* M2

[21] SECOND MODE, THE SUBORDINATE OF THE FIRST

[Ex. 3]

No-   e-a-is

[22] Following is the intonation, which ascends to the fourth degree of the terminal tetrachord and descends to the fourth degree of the lowest tetrachord, ranging over five scale-steps:

[Ex. 4]

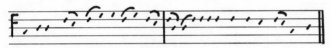

Gloria... et nunc et semper et in secula seculorum amen

[A]   Ma-   gnum

23 TONUS TERTIUS, ID EST AUCTORALIS SECUNDUS

[Ex. 5]

𝄞𝄢 musical notation

No- e-a- no-e- a-ne

24 Sequitur modulatio psalmi eleuata in tetrardum superiorem in septem complexa sonis:'

P 2v
Bg 44v

[Ex. 6]

	nunc			
		et per	lo	
	a et	sem e n secula secu	m	
	ri	i	rv a	
	Glo	t	me	
			n	

[A] Qui de ter-ra est de ter-ra lo-qui- tvr

---

23 tercius Bg // tritus M2 P1 P2 // auctoraris *cor in* auctoralis M2
Ex. 5: Noe-o- noeane Bg
om C M2 P1 P2
neuma: [notation] [ ] [notation] ·

P

Ex. 6: [secu]lo-rum amen C
psalmum om M2
not psalmi men P1 P2
qui de terra [est de terra loquitur] *s n* Bg
loquitur C
Qui de terra de terra est de terra loquitur [*sic*] *s n* M2
terra loquitur <qui de caelo uenit super omnes est> P1 P2

[23] THIRD MODE, THAT IS, SECOND AUTHENTIC

[Ex. 5]

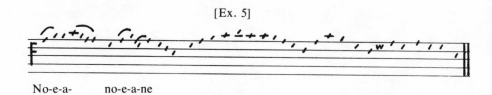

No-e-a-   no-e-a-ne

[24] Following is the intonation, which reaches the fourth degree of the upper tetrachord, encompassing seven scale-steps:

[Ex. 6]

Gloria... et nunc et semper et in secula seculorum amen

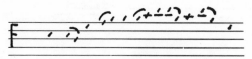

[A]   Qui de ter-ra est de ter-ra lo-qui-tur

[25] SEQUITUR TONUS QUARTUS SUBIUGALIS TERTII

[Ex. 7]

ƒIƒƒƒ ⊿ Iƒ ƒIƒ·IIƒ·[I] ƒ˥·ƒ⁓Iƒ·IƒIƒ·
No-   e-a- is

[26] Sequitur modvlatio psalmi erecta in devtervm
superiorem:'

W 83v
P2 51

[Ex. 8]

		nc et	m				rv	
	a e	u	se per e	n secula seculo	m			
	ri	t nu		t i			a	
		u	fra					
	Glo	s a tem uos		s			me	
	ne		tres	es				
	[A] Om				tis'		n	C 53v

---

[25] tercii Bg P1 P2
[27] ID EST: idem Bg // tertius M2 P1

Ex. 7: *Neuma*: *ƒIƒ IIƒ⁓ƒ˥ƒ⁓IƒIƒIƒ*   Bg
ƒIƒ   *ƒIƒIIƒIƒƒIIƒ*
No-   eagis   *(require hoc exemplum sub sequentem titulum)* C
Noeagis *s n* M2 P1 P2
              ⊿ʒ   ƥʒ
Ex. 8: nunc Bg *not men* C P1 P2 // nunc C P1 Ps // *psalmum om* M2 // Omnes
autem uos fratres estis *s n* M2 P1 P2 // et patres *add s n post* estis P1 P2

C

25 FOURTH MODE, THE SUBORDINATE OF THE THIRD

[Ex. 7]

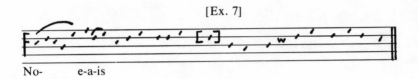

No-   e-a-is

26 Following is the intonation, which rises to the second degree of the upper tetrachord:

[Ex. 8]

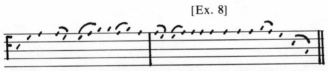

Gloria... et nunc et semper et in secula seculorum a-men

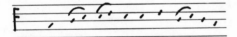

[A]   Om-nes au-tem vos fra-tres estis

[27] SEQUITUR TONUS QUINTUS, ID EST AUCTORALIS TERCIUS

[Ex. 9]

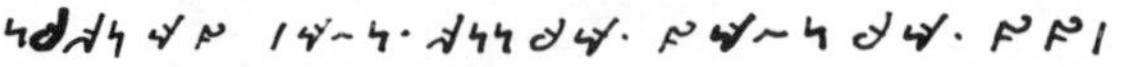

No- e-a-ne

[28] Sequitur modulatio psalmi, quae erigitvr usque in tetrardum superiorem sex conclusa sonis:' Pl 37v

[Ex. 10]

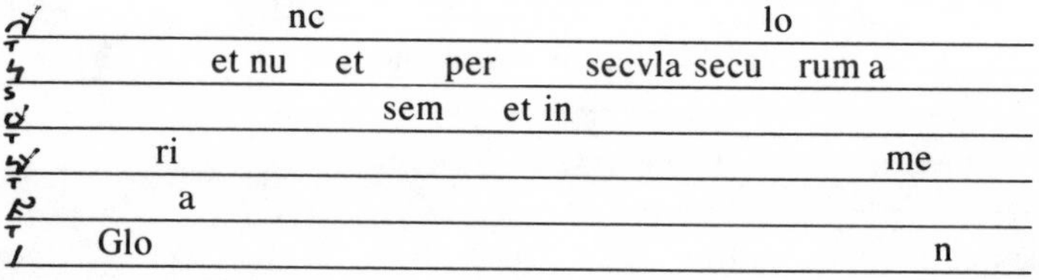

nc lo
et nu et per secvla secu rum a
sem et in
ri me
a
Glo n

[A] Pa-ga-no-rum mul-ti-tu-do fu-gi-ens ad se-pul-chrum' Bg 45 P 3

---

[28] Sequitur... sonis *om* Bg //erigitvr: eruntur C // tetrardum: tetrardum tetrardi C P1 P2 W // tetrardi P // tetrardum *cor in marg in* tetrardum tetrardi M2 // superiorum C P W

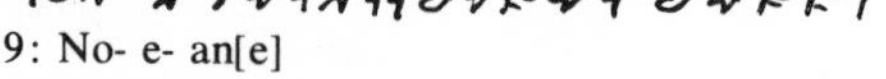

Ex. 9: No- e- an[e] C

Om M2

neuma: 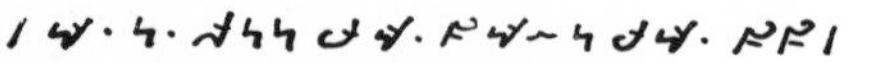 P W

No- e- ane P1

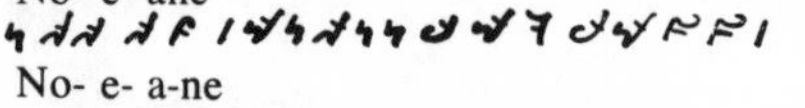

No- e- a-ne P2

Ex. 10: [nu]nc Bg // seculorum amen C // *om* M2 // *not men* P1 P2 // Paganorum multitudo *s n* Bg // *antiphonam om* C P1 P2 // sepul[chrum] P // [A] Uox clamantis 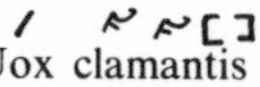 *add* C // Vox clamantis *add in marg* PW 

27 FIFTH MODE, THAT IS, THIRD AUTHENTIC

[Ex. 9]

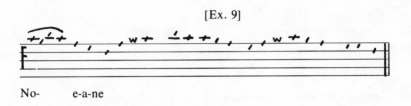

No-   e-a-ne

28 Following is the intonation, which rises to the fourth degree of the upper tetrachord, enclosing six scale-steps:

[Ex. 10]

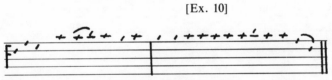

Gloria... et nunc et semper et in secula seculorum a-men

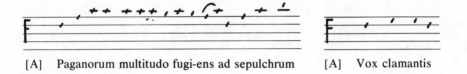

[A]   Paganorum multitudo fugi-ens ad sepulchrum   [A]   Vox clamantis

²⁹ TONUS SEXTUS SUBIUGALIS QUINTI

[Ex. 11]

//ᴘ✦ᴘ /· /⁻ ᴘ⁊· /ᴘ ✦· ᴘᴘ/ ·

An- ne

³⁰ Sequitur modulatio psalmi, sonis consistens quatuor:

[Ex. 12]

	nc						
	a et nu	et se	per		n secula secu		m
	ri		m	et	in		lorv a
	Glo			t			men

³¹ SEQUITUR TONUS SEPTIMUS ID EST AUCTORALIS QUARTUS

[Ex. 13]

✦⁊⁊ ✦⁊ ✦ ᴘ✦⁻⁊ ·✦⁊⁊✦✦ᴘ/ · ✦⁻⁊✦✦✦✦ ✦ᴘ

No- e-a-ne

---

²⁹ sextus *om* M2 // QUINTIM W

³⁰ psalmi *om* C M2 P1 P2

Ex. 11: Ann[e] *//ᴘ⁊✦ᴘᴘᴘ/*   C

om M2

del P1

//ᴘ✦ᴘ //ᴘ⁊ /ᴘ✦ ᴘ✦ᴘᴘ/
[Anne]   P2

Ex. 12: seculorum Bg // Gloria et nunc (et) semper et C // *om* M2 // (semper)
et P // Gloria et nunc [et] sem-per et in P1 P2

[A] O quam *add s n in marg* Bg P W

[29] SIXTH MODE, THE SUBORDINATE OF THE FIFTH

[Ex. 11]

An-   ne

[30] Following is the intonation, consisting of four scale-steps:

[Ex. 12]

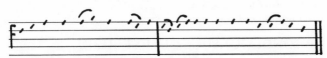

Gloria... et nunc et semper et in secula seculorum amen

[A]   O   quam[3]

[31] FOLLOWING IS THE SEVENTH MODE, THAT IS, FOURTH AUTHENTIC

[Ex. 13]

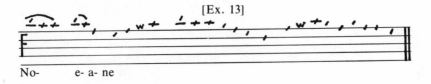

No-   e- a- ne

---

[3]   The cue is completed from HARTKER, *Codex (ed. cit.)*, 331.
    [ ]
    Ex. 13: No[e]ane   C
om M2

No-   ea-ne   P
del P1
No[e]ane   P2

No-   eane   W

³² Sequitvr modulatio psalmi elevata usque in devterum excellentem:'

term hic
C M2 P1 P2

[Ex. 14]

𝄢		nc				
		et se	per		lo	
	a et nu		m	et n secula secu	rvm	
	Glori			t i		a
						men

[A] Ioseph fili Dauid noli timere accipere

³³ SEQUITUR TONUS OCTAUUS QUI EST SUBIU-GALIS SEPTIMI'

W 84

[Ex. 15]

[No-e-a- is]

³⁴ Sequitur modvlatio psalmi pertingens ad quartvm tetracordi superioris:'

Bg 45v

[Ex. 16]

𝄢		nc et	m				
	e nu		se	pe e	n secula secu	rvm	
	t		r		lo	m	
	ria			t i		a	
	Glo					men	

[A] Per uis-ce-ra mi-sericor-di-e Dei nostri'

P 3v

---

³² isque C // excellente P2
³³ octauus tonus Bg

Ex. 14: *Not men* Bg // a-men Bg // Ioseph fili Dauid *s n* Bg //

[A] Svb thro-no   [Dei] *add in marg* P W
    Ex. 15: *om* Bg
    Ex. 16: nu[n]c P // Per uiscera misericordie dei nostri *s n* Bg

[32] Following is the intonation, which rises to the second degree of the highest tetrachord:

[Ex. 14]

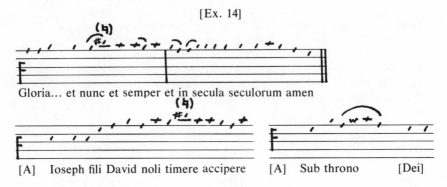

Gloria... et nunc et semper et in secula seculorum amen

[A]   Ioseph fili David noli timere accipere   [A]   Sub throno   [Dei]

[33] FOLLOWING IS THE EIGHTH MODE, THE SUBORDINATE OF THE SEVENTH

[Ex. 15]

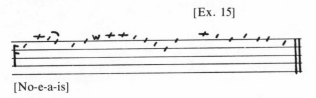

[No-e-a-is]

[34] Following is the intonation, which reaches the fourth degree of the upper tetrachord:

[Ex. 16]

Gloria... et nunc et semper et in   secula seculorum amen

[A]   Per viscera misericordie Dei nostri[4]

---

[4]   HARTKER, 423.

[35] Hae sunt modulationes quas ad antiphonas accipimus octo tonorum, quae ordinem acceperunt ab ordine sonorum sursum numeratorum. [36] Quas tamen modulationes ubi morosiori cantu est opus, utpote ad cantica euangeliorum, cum ad hoc uacat, secundum quod superius expressum est, assumere solemus. [37] Porro ad cursvm canendum isdem quidem, sed expeditioribus melodiis utimur, quas nihilominus in hac subiecta notatione significare curaui. [38] Noeane [etc.] uero non sunt uerba aliquid significantia, sed syllabae ad inuestigandam melodiam aptae.

[39] PRIMUS TONUS

[Ex. 17]

Beati inmaculati in uia *qui ambulant in le-ge Do-mini

[40] SECUNDUS TONUS

[Ex. 18]

Beati qui scrutantur testimonia eius

*in toto corde exqui- runt e-vm

---

[35] quae: qui Bg P W // ordinem: ordinem ab ordinem P W
[37] cursim Bg // cursim *cor in* cursvm W
[38] Noane P W // inuestigandum *cor in* inuestigandam P
[40-46] TONUS *om* Bg

Ex. 17: Bea-ti Bg // inmacula-ti P W

Ex. 18: testimonia P W // e-um Bg

[35] These are, for antiphons, the accepted intonations, which take the disposition of the eight modes in respect of the arrangement of the scale-steps classified above. [36] These intonations, as was indicated earlier, are customarily used where the performance of a chant is slower, as for instance for the Gospel Canticles, when time allows. [37] The very same melodies, sung more quickly, are also used for the faster chants, which, nevertheless, I have taken care to indicate in the following table. [38] *Noeane* [and the rest] are not in fact words with any meaning, but rather syllables intended for investigating [the structure of] melody.

[39] FIRST MODE

[Ex. 17]

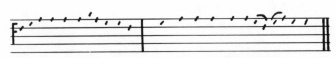

Beati inmaculati in via   qui ambulant in lege Domini

[40] SECOND MODE

[Ex. 18]

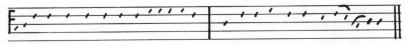

Beati qui scrutantur testimonia eius   in toto corde exquirunt eum

41 TERTIUS TONUS

[Ex. 19]

Non enim qui operantur iniquitatem

*in uiis eius ambula-ue-runt

42 QUARTUS TONUS

[Ex. 20]

Tu mandasti mandata tua *custodiri ni-mis

43 QUINTUS TONUS

[Ex. 21]

Utinam dirigantur uiae meae

*ad custodiendas iustificationes tu-as

44 SEXTUS TONUS

[Ex. 22]

Tunc non confundar dum perspicio *in omnia manda-ta tu-a'   Bg 46

Ex. 19: eius am-bulauerunt Bg P W

Ex. 20: tua <domine> custodiri Bg // custodiri P

Ex. 21: viae meae Bg P // uiae mee W

Ex. 22: dum P W // respicio Bg // tu- a Bg

[41] THIRD MODE

[Ex. 19]

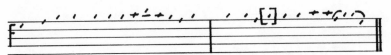

Non enim qui operantur iniquitatem   in viis eius ambulaverunt

[42] FOURTH MODE

[Ex. 20]

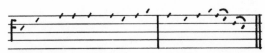

Tu mandasti mandata tua   custodiri nimis

[43] FIFTH MODE

[Ex. 21]

Utinam dirigantur viae meae   ad custodiendas iustificationes tuas

[44] SIXTH MODE

[Ex. 22]

Tunc non confundar dum perspicio   in omnia mandata tua

45 SEPTIMUS TONUS

[Ex. 23]

Confitebor tibi Domine in directione cordis

*quod didici iudicia tv-a

46 OCTAUUS TONUS

[Ex. 24]

Iustificationes tuas custodiam

*non me derelinquas us-que-qua-que'   P 4

47 Extra has quoque ad plerosque desupradictis tonis et aliae psalmorum modulationes aptantur, utpote ad antiphonas istas: Benedicta tv in mulieribus et Ex Egypto uocaui filium mevm et reliquas his similes, quae secundo deputan'dae sunt tono quae per duos diuersos modos W 84v alternatim valent inter choros cantari, ut suo modo unus chorus suum uersum pronuntiat et alter alio modo respondeat:

[Ex. 25]

[A] Benedic-ta tu in mv-li-eribus et bene-dic-tus fructus

uentris tui

---

47   antiphones P W // in mulieribus et *om* Bg // egipto P // meum *om* Bg // (simi-les) que P W // deputatae Bg // pronunciat Bg

Ex. 23: cordis <in eo> quod didici iudicia tu-a Bg

Ex. 25: fructus P mulieribus Bg // tu-i *(neuma om)* Bg

45 SEVENTH MODE

[Ex. 23]

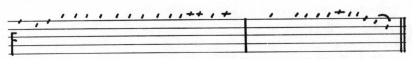

Confitebor tibi domine in directione cordis   quod didici iudicia tua

46 EIGHTH MODE

[Ex. 24]

Iustificationes tuas custodiam   non me derelinquas usquequaque

47 In addition to these psalm intonations, which are suitable in most instances for the modes mentioned above, there are others which may be used. In the case of the antiphons *Benedicta tu in mulieribus, Ex Egypto vocavi filium meum* and others like them which are assigned to the second mode, the psalm intonations are to be sung by the choirs in two contrasting ways alternately — one chorus singing its verse in one manner and the other responding differently:

[Ex. 25]

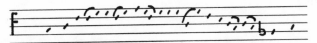

[A]   Benedicta tu in mulieribus et benedictus fructus

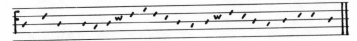

ventris tui

[ƒ] ⌐ ⌐ ⌐

Be- nedictus Dominus Deus Israel

*quia uisitauit et fecit redemptionem plebis su-ae

Et erexit cornu salutis nobis

*in domo Dauid pueri su-i

48 Item tono sexto hoc quoque modo psalmi ad antiphonas modulantur:

[Ex. 26]

[A] Notum fecit Dominus alleluia

Can-ta-te Domino canticum no-uum

*quia mirabilia fecit Dominus

Sal-ua-uit sibi dextera e-ius *et brachium sanctum e-ius

No-tum fe-cit Dominus salutare su-um

[⌐]

*ante conspectvm gentium reuelauit iustitiam suam

et reliqua.

---

48 antiphonam Bg // et reliqua *om* Bg

Benedictus Bg P W // domi-nus P W // israhel Bg // is-rahel P // is- rael W // suae Bg
// nobis P W

Ex. 26: cantate *cor in* can-ta-te *in marg* W // saluabit P // dexteram P W //
salutarum P // iusticiam P // Notum fecit dominus salutare... suam *om* Bg

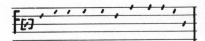

Benedictus Dominus Deus Israel

quia visitavit et fecit redemptionem   plebis suae

Et erexit cornu salutis nobis   in domo David pueri sui

⁴⁸ Similarly, for [certain] antiphons of the sixth mode, this is another way of singing the psalm:

[Ex. 26]

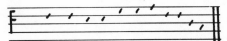

[A]   Notum fecit Dominus alleluia

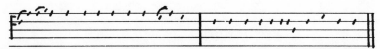

Cantate Domino canticum novum   quia mirabilia fecit Dominus

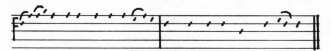

Salvavit sibi dextera eius   et brachium sanctum eius

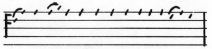

Notum fecit dominus salutare suum

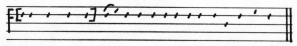

ante conspectum gentium revelavit iustitiam suam

and so forth.

⁴⁹ Sunt etiam propriae ad quasdam antiphonas modulationes suae,' sicut in hac secundi toni antiphona: Bg 46v

[Ex. 27]

[A]   Ani-ma mea exultabit in Do-mino delectabitur in salu-ta-ri suo

Iudica Domine no-cen-tes me   *expugna inpugnantes me

Adprehende arma et scutum   *et exurge in adiutorium mihi

Effunde frameam et conclude aduersus eos qui me' persequuntur P 4v

*dic animae meae salus tua ego sum

et cetera.

⁵⁰ Item ad tonum nouissimvm:

[Ex. 28]

[A]   In templo Do-mi-ni omnes di-cent glori-am

Af-fer-te Domino filii Dei   *afferte Domino filios a-rietvm

---

⁴⁹   proprie W // Sicut P W // sicut in hac secundi toni antiphona om Bg // et cetera om Bg

Ex. 27: (exultabit) in P //domino Bg // nocentes Bg (nocentes) me Bg P W // ex-pugna Bg P W // adprehende P // scutum Bg P W // et (exurge) P W // exurge in adiutorium P // me persecuntur Bg // me persecuntur dic anime mee P //me persequntur [sic] W // anima mea Bg

[49] There are still other intonations peculiar to certain antiphons, as for the following antiphon of the second mode:

[Ex. 27]

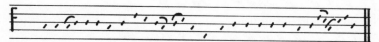

[A]   Anima mea exultabit in Domino delectabitur in salutari suo

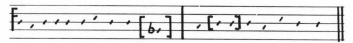

Judica Domine nocentes me   expugna inpugnantes me

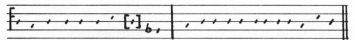

Adprehende arma et scutum   et exurge in adiutorium mihi

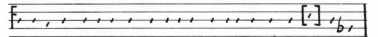

Effunde frameam et conclude adversus eos qui me persequuntur

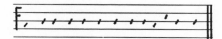

dic animae meae salus tua ego sum

and so on.

[50] Similarly for [this antiphon of] the last mode:

[Ex. 28]

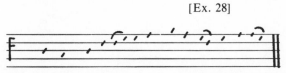

[A]   In templo Domini omnes dicent gloriam

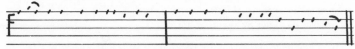

Afferte Domino filii Dei   afferte Domino filios arietum

⁵¹ Similiter ad antiphonas:

[Ex. 29]

[A]   Nos qui ui-ui-mus benedicimus Do-minum

[A]   Martyres Do-mi-ni Dominum benedicite in ae-ternum

et alia huiusmodi, siqua sunt.

⁵² Preterea pro diuersitate antiphonarum quae psalmis adiunguntur, per omnes pene octo tonorum melodias finis uersuum uariatur, quarum diuersitatum in primo tono hae formae sunt:

⁵³ Primus Modus:

[Ex. 30]

Gloria seculo-rum amen

[A]   Ecce no-men Do-mi-ni

---

⁵¹   et siqua sint alia huiusmodi Bg
⁵³   *titulum om* Bg // MODUS: TONUS P W

Ex. 28: Adferte Bg // filii Bg // adferte Bg

Ex. 29: Item *add inter antiphonas* Bg // domini P W // aeternum P W
Ex. 30: Ecce nomen domini *s n* Bg

[51] Also for these antiphons:

[Ex. 29]

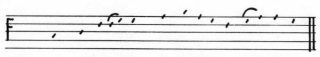

[A]   Nos qui vivimus   benedicimus   Dominum

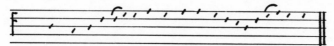

[A]   Martyres Domini Dominum benedicite in aeternum

and others of the same sort if, in fact, there are any.

[52] Furthermore, because of the diversity of the antiphons associated with psalms, the verse endings of nearly all of the eight [regular] melodies are variable. The variations take the following forms in the first mode.

[53] First Manner:

[Ex. 30]

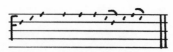

Gloria... seculorum amen

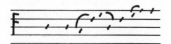

[A]   Ecce nomen Domini

⁵⁴ Secundus [Modus]:

[Ex. 31]

♦♦♦ ♪/ ♪ ♪/♪♪
Seculo-rum a-men

[A]   Euge serue bone'   *term*
                                                          Bg

⁵⁵ Tertius [Modus]:

[Ex. 32]

♦ ♦♦ ♪/ ♪♦
Secu-lo-rum amen

[A]   Apertis thesauris suis

⁵⁶ Quartus Modus:

[Ex. 33]

♦♦♦ ♪/ ♪ ♪♦♪
Secu-lo-rum a-men

[A]   Sol et luna

---

⁵⁴   *titulum om* Bg
⁵⁶   MODUS: TONUS P W
          ♪♪♪♪ ♪
Ex. 31: <Gloria> seculorum Bg

Ex. 32: tesauris P

54 Second Manner:

[Ex. 31]

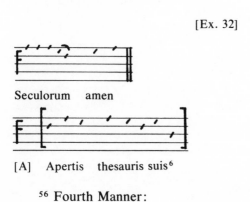

Seculorum   amen

[A]   E-   u- ge serve bone[5]

55 Third Manner:

[Ex. 32]

Seculorum   amen

[A]   Apertis   thesauris suis[6]

56 Fourth Manner:

[Ex. 33]

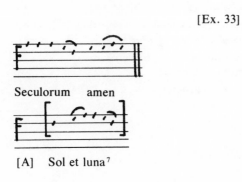

Seculorum   amen

[A]   Sol et luna[7]

---

5   Cf. Ex. 2.
6   HARTKER, 76.
7   HARTKER, 95.

⁵⁷ Similiter et medietates seu distinctiones in uersibus pro diuersa positione uerborum diuerse habent. ⁵⁸ Exempli causa primus modus:

[Ex. 34]

Eructauit cor meum uerbum bonum   *dico ego

Propterea benedixit te Deus in aeternum   *accingere [gladio]

Myrra et gutta et casia a uestimentis tuis   *a gradibus

⁵⁹ Secundus Modus:

[Ex. 35]

Lingua mea calamus scribe   *uelociter [scribentis]

Speciem tuam et pulchritvdinem tuam intende   *[prospere]

Dilexisti iusticiam et odisti iniquitatem   *propterea

---

⁵⁷   diuers[a] P // dispositione P

Ex. 34: eternum W
Ex. 35: pulchritvdinem P W

[57] There are, as well, similarly differing median cadences or divisions within the verses, owing to the varying disposition of the words.

[58] First Manner:

[Ex. 34]

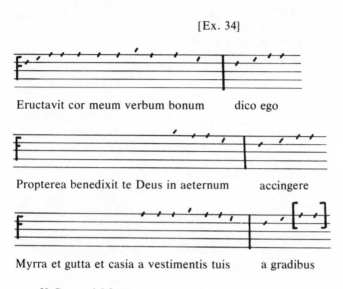

Eructavit cor meum verbum bonum   dico ego

Propterea benedixit te Deus in aeternum   accingere

Myrra et gutta et casia a vestimentis tuis   a gradibus

[59] Second Manner:

[Ex. 35]

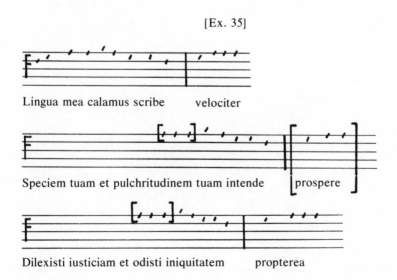

Lingua mea calamus scribe   velociter

Speciem tuam et pulchritudinem tuam intende   prospere

Dilexisti iusticiam et odisti iniquitatem   propterea

⁶⁰ Tertius **Modus**:

[Ex. 36]

[neume notation]

Speciosus forma pre filiis hominum   *diffusa

[neume notation]

Sedes tua Deus in seculum seculi   *[uirga]

⁶¹ Quartus **Modus**:

[Ex. 37]

[neume notation]

Propter ueritatem et mansuetvdinem et iusticiam'   *et dedisti   P 5

Sagittae tuae acutae potentissimae   *populi

⁶² Quintus **Modus**:

[Ex. 38]

Nam et testimonia tva meditatio mea est   *et consolatio

⁶³ Sextus **Modus**:

[exemplum vacat]

_____

Ex. 37: tue W

⁶⁰ Third Manner:

[Ex. 36]

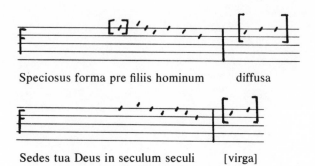

Speciosus forma pre filiis hominum   diffusa

Sedes tua Deus in seculum seculi   [virga]

⁶¹ Fourth Manner:

[Ex. 37]

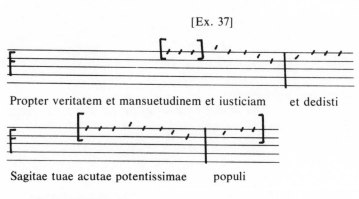

Propter veritatem et mansuetudinem et iusticiam   et dedisti

Sagitae tuae acutae potentissimae   populi

⁶² Fifth Manner:

[Ex. 38]

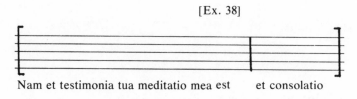

Nam et testimonia tua meditatio mea est   et consolatio

⁶³ Sixth Manner:

[example missing]

⁶⁴ [SECUNDUS TONUS]

[Ex. 39]

Gloria seculorum amen

⁶⁵ Primus **Modus**:

[Ex. 40]

Dies diei eructat uerbum   *et nox nocti indicat scientiam

Desiderabilia super aurum' et lapidem preciosum multum   W 85

*et dulciora

Si mei non fuerint dominati tunc inmaculatus ero

*et emundabor

Et erunt ut complaceant eloquia oris mei   *et meditatio

⁶⁶ Secundus **Modus**:

[Ex. 41]

Caeli enarrant gloriam Dei   *et opera

Ex. 40: eructvat W // emundabor P

Ex. 41: custodiendo P // dies W // episcopatum P

[64] [SECOND MODE]

[Ex. 39]

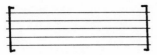

Gloria... seculorum amen

[65] First Manner:

[Ex. 40]

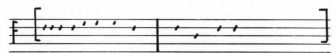

Dies diei eructat verbum   et nox nocti indicat scientiam

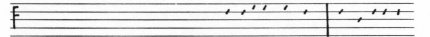

Desiderabilia super aurum et lapidem preciosum multum   et dulciora

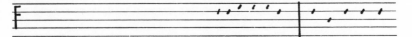

Si mei non fuerint dominati tunc inmaculatus ero   et emundabor

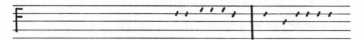

Et erunt ut complaceant eloquia oris mei   et meditatio

[66] Second Manner:

[Ex. 41]

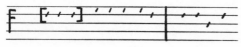

Caeli enarrant gloriam Dei   et opera

♪ ♪♪♪ ♪♪   ♪ ♪ ♪♪ ♪ ♪

Nam et seruus tuus custodiet ea   *in custodiendo

♪♪ ♪♪ ♪♪   ♪ ♪ ♪♪ ♪♪♪

Fiant dies eius pauci   *et episcopatum

⁶⁷ Tertius **Modus**:

[Ex. 42]

♪   ♪ ♪ ♪♪♪ ♪♪   ♪ ♪♪ ♪

Magna est gloria eius in salutari tuo   *gloriam

♪ ♪ ♪♪♪ ♪♪   ♪ ♪♪ ♪

Inuenietur manus tua omnibus inimicis tuis   *dextera

⁶⁸ Quartus **Modus**:

[Ex. 43]

[♪♪ ♪♪] ♪♪ ♪♪ ♪

Non sunt loquelae neque sermones

♪ ♪   ♪ ♪♪ ♪ ♪♪♪ ♪ ♪

*quorum non audientur uerba

♪♪ ♪♪ ♪♪   ♪♪ ♪

Quoniam alieni insurgunt in me et fortes quesierunt animam meam

♪ ♪   ♪ ♪♪♪ ♪♪♪ ♪

*et non proposuerunt Deum

Ex. 43: in me *bis* P

Nam et servus tuus custodiet ea   in custodiendo

Fiant dies eius pauci   et episcopatum

[67] Third Manner:

[Ex. 42]

Magna est gloria eius in salutari tuo   gloriam

Invenietur manus tua omnibus inimicis tuis   dextera

[68] Fourth Manner:

[Ex. 43]

Non sunt loquelae neque sermones   quorum non audientur verba

Quoniam alieni insurgunt in me et fortes quesierunt animam meam

et non proposuerunt Deum

⁶⁹ Quintus **Modus**:

[Ex. 44]

Lex Domini inreprehensibilis conuertens animas

*testimonium

Iustitiae Domini rectae letificantes corda

*preceptum Domini

⁷⁰ Sextus **Modus**:

[Ex. 45]

Domine in uirtute tua laetabitur rex   *et super salutare

Deus Deus meus respice in me   *[quare me]

⁷¹ Sunt preterea multa quae conferri magis quam scribi oportet, quae scilicet in principiis uel in distinctionibus et membris uersuum pro accentuum aut euphoniae ratione obseruanda sunt. ⁷²Accentuum dumtaxat ut melo Dorio canens dicat:'

P 5v

[Ex. 46]

Si reddidi retribuentibus mihi mala   *decidam merito

---

⁷¹   euphonie W

Ex. 44: testimonium P // Iusticiae P // laetificantes P // preceptum P

Ex. 45: tua *om* P // salutare *om* P // respice P W in (me) *om* W

⁶⁹ Fifth Manner:

[Ex. 44]

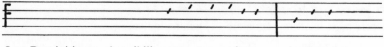

Lex Domini inreprehensibilis convertens animas   testimonium

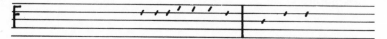

Iustitiae Domini rectae letificantes corda   preceptum Domini

⁷⁰ Sixth Manner:

[Ex. 45]

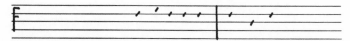

Domine in virtute tua laetabitur rex   et super salutare

Deus Deus meus respice in me   [quare me]

⁷¹ There are many things in addition which — more readily applied than described — are to be observed for the beginnings, medians and body of the verses, for reasons of accent and euphony. ⁷²As far as the accent is concerned, the singing of a Dorian melody should be as follows:

[Ex. 46]

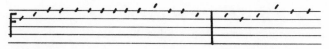

Si reddidi retribuentibus mihi mala   decidam merito

⁷³ uel inferiore:

[Ex. 47]

Et propter hanc in altum regredere   *Domine iudica

⁷⁴ uel ita potius:

[Ex. 48]

Diligam te Domine uirtus mea   *Dominus firmamentum

⁷⁵ Item:

[Ex. 49]

Saluum me fac Domine quoniam defecit sanctus

*quoniam diminutae

⁷⁶ Quamuis super doctus quisque superuacuae am-
monetur.

⁷⁷ Item pro euphoniae causa, ut ibi in distinguendo
uocales [quae] coeunt hiatus quantum ualet uitetur, vt:

[Ex. 50]

Ego autem sum uermis et non homo   *opprobrium hominum

_____

⁷⁶ superuacue W
⁷⁷ euphonie W // uocale P

Ex. 49: diminutae: deminñ W

⁷³ Or, for the plagal:

[Ex. 47]

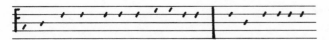

Et propter hanc in altum regredere   Domine iudica

⁷⁴ Another example, in the authentic:

[Ex. 48]

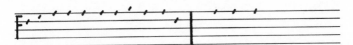

Diligam te Domine virtus mea   Dominus firmamentum

⁷⁵ Another:

[Ex. 49]

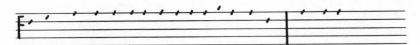

Salvum me fac Domine quoniam defecit sanctus   quoniam diminutae

⁷⁶ It is to be noted however that these examples are superfluous for experienced singers.

⁷⁷ For the sake of euphony, when articulating juxtaposed vowels as in the following, a hiatus is to be avoided at all costs:

[Ex. 50]

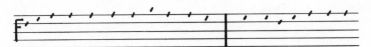

Ego autem sum vermis et non homo   opprobrium hominum

Ꝛ ꝑ /   /   / /   / ꝑꝑ ꝑ /   / ꝑ / / /

Exurge Domine in ira tua   *et exaltare

/ ꝑ✔   ✔ ✔ ✔ ✔   ♩   ✔ ✔ ꝑ

Exurge Domine Deus meus in precepto quod mandasti

ꝑ / ꝑ ✔ ✔

*et synagoga

Ꝛ ꝑ / /   / ꝑꝑꝑ /   /

Corripuit me iustvs in misericordia et increpauit me

/ ꝑ /   /   /

*oleum autem

78 Pro euphonia quoque siue colis:

[Ex. 51]

/   ꝑ✔   ✔ ✔ ♩ ✔ ꝑ✔ꝑ /   ✔ ✔ ✔ ✔ ꝑꝑ ♩ ✔ ✔

Et propter hanc in altum regredere   *Domine iudica populos

Ꝛ   ꝑ [/]   /   ꝑꝑ ꝑ /

Arcum suum tetendit et parauit eum

ꝑ / / / [/]   / ꝑ   ꝑ /

*et in ipso parauit vasa mortis

/ / / ꝑ /

sagitas suas

/ ꝑ   ✔✔✔✔✔✔♩✔ ✔ꝑ   / ♩✔✔✔

Lacum aperuit et effodit eum   *et incidit in foueam

Ꝛ ꝑ[/]   / / /   / ꝑꝑꝑ ꝑ /

Confitemini Domino secundum iustitiam eius

ꝑ   ꝑ /

*et psallam nomini Domini

Ex. 50: (hominum) Exsurge P // exaltare P // (exaltare) Exsurge P // synagoga
P // oleum P

Ex. 51: (et) pa-rauit P W // Confitemini P // iusticiam P

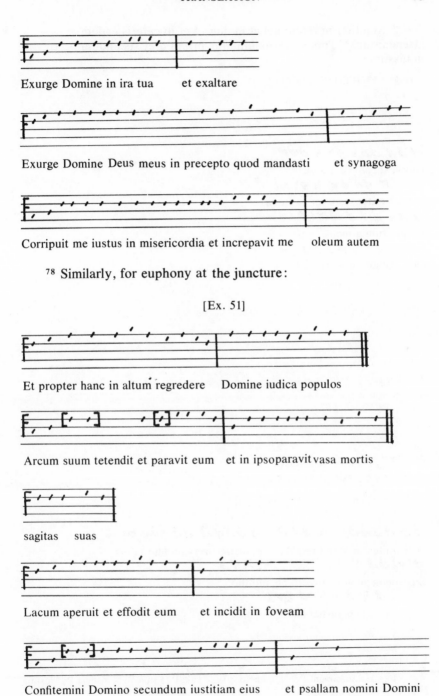

Exurge Domine in ira tua   et exaltare

Exurge Domine Deus meus in precepto quod mandasti   et synagoga

Corripuit me iustus in misericordia et increpavit me   oleum autem

[78] Similarly, for euphony at the juncture:

[Ex. 51]

Et propter hanc in altum regredere   Domine iudica populos

Arcum suum tetendit et paravit eum   et in ipsoparavit vasa mortis

sagitas   suas

Lacum aperuit et effodit eum   et incidit in foveam

Confitemini Domino secundum iustitiam eius   et psallam nomini Domini

⁷⁹ Similiter in tercio uel et in quarto et in ceteris eadem attendantur. ⁸⁰ Tonus sextus imitatur primum et secundum nouissimus.

⁸¹ [TERTIUS TONUS]

[Ex. 52]

Gloria seculo-rum a-men

[A]   Tv Bet-leem ter-ra Iu-da

Seculo-rum a-men

[A]   Quan-do na-tus est

⁸² [Primus Modus:]

[Ex. 53]

Deus iudicium tvum regi da   *et iusticiam tvam filio re-gis

Suscipiant montes pacem populo tuo

*et colles iustici-am'

P 6
W 85v

Ex. 53: Suscipiant P W // populo P W // su-a P // su-a W // iusticia P // iustitia W

[79] The same things hold for the third, fourth and for the other modes. [80] The sixth mode is like the first, and the last like the second.

[81] [THIRD MODE]

[Ex. 52]

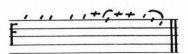

Gloria... seculorum amen

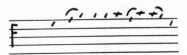

[A]   Tu Betleem terra Iuda

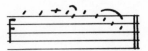

Seculorum amen

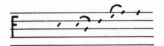

[A]   Quando natus est

[82] [First Manner:]

[Ex. 53]

Deus iudicium tuum regi da   et iusticiam tuam filio regis

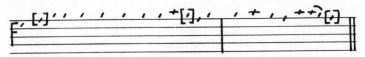

Suscipiant montes pacem populo tuo   et colles iusticiam

In sua iustitia iudicabit pauperes huius populi

*et saluos faciet filios pau-pe-rvm

83 Secundus Modus:

[Ex. 54]

Et humiliabit calumniatorem

*et permanebit cum sole et ante lunam

in seculum se-cu-li

Et descendit sicut pluuia in uellus

*et sicut stillicidia stillantia super terram

Et uiuet et dabitur ei de auro Arabie

*et adorabunt de ipso semper tota die

benedicent

Ex. 54: *not saepissime dubia* P W // humiliauit P // humiliabit W // calumniatorem P W (Pluuia) in P W // stillicidia stillantia P W //super terram *s n* P W // adorabunt
P // magna *in marg* W // solus magna P // misericordiam P W

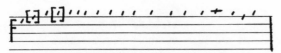

In sua iustitia iudicabit pauperes huius populi

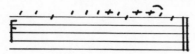

et salvos faciet filios pauperum

⁸³ Second Manner:

[Ex. 54]

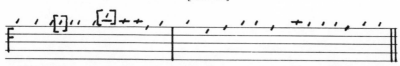

Et humiliabit calumniatorem   et permanebit cum sole et ante lunam

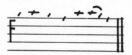

in seculum seculi

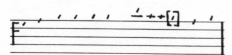

Et descendit sicut   pluvia in   vellus

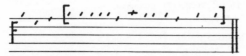

et sicut stillicidia stillantia super terram

Et vivet et dabitur ei de auro Arabie   et adorabunt de ipso semper tota die

benedicent

Benedictus Dominus Deus Israhel qui facit mirabilia magna solus

*et benedictum nomen maiestatis eius　*in aeternum

in seculum seculi

Hic accipiet benedictionem a Domino

*et misericordiam a Deo

[84] Tertius Modus:

[Ex. 55]

Coram illo procident Ethiopes　*et inimici

Reges Tharsis et insule munera offerent　*reges Arabum

Parcet pauperi et inopi　*et animas pauperum

Ex. 55: ethyopes P //mune-ra P

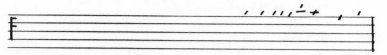

Benedictus Dominus Deus Israhel qui facit mirabilia magna solus

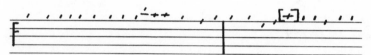

et benedictum nomen maiestatis eius   in aeternum

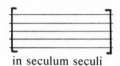

in seculum seculi

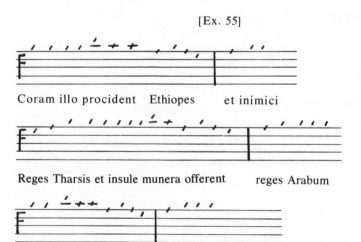

Hic accipiet benedictionem a Domino   et misericordiam a Deo

[84] Third Manner:

[Ex. 55]

Coram illo procident   Ethiopes   et inimici

Reges Tharsis et insule munera offerent   reges Arabum

Parcet pauperi et inopi   et animas pauperum

85 QUARTUS TONUS

[Ex. 56]

Gloria seculorum a-men

[A]   Innuebant pa-tri e-ius

Seculorum a-men

[A]   Uigilate animo

Seculorum amen

[A]   Hymnum dicite

Seculo-rum a-men

[A]   Om-nes au-tem uos frat-res es-tis

Ex. 56: a-men (Innuebant) P // Innuebant: Innueniebant P

[85] FOURTH MODE

[Ex. 56]

Gloria... seculorum amen

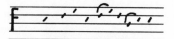

[A]   Innuebant patri eius

Seculorum amen

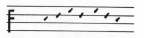

[A]   V igilate animo . .

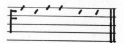

Seculorum amen

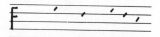

[A]   Hymnum   dicite

Seculorum amen

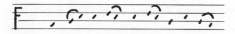

[A]   Omnes autem vos fratres estis

Seculo-rum a-men

[A]   Lau-da-bo Deum me-um

86 Primus Modus:

[Ex. 57]

Dies diei eructat uerbum   *et nox nocti

Desiderium super aurum et lapidem pretiosum multvm

*[et dulciora]

[P]

Si mei non fuerint dominati tunc inmaculatus ero

*et e-mvndabor

87 Secundus Modus:

[Ex. 58]

[F]

Caeli enarrant gloriam Dei   *et opera manuum

[F]

Nam et seruus tuus custodiet ea   *in custodiendo illa

Ex. 57: e-ruc-tat P // eructat *cor in* eructvat W // preciosum P // Si P W // in-

macula-tus P W

Ex. 58: Caeli P W // de-i P W // Nam P W

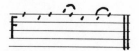

Seculorum amen

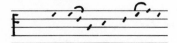

[A]   Laudabo Deum meum

[86] First Manner:

[Ex. 57]

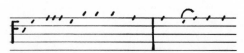

Dies diei eructat verbum   et nox nocti

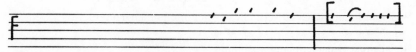

Desiderium super aurum et lapidem pretiosum multum   [et dulciora]

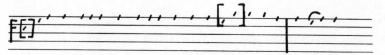

Si mei non fuerint dominati tunc inmaculatus ero   et emundabor

[87] Second Manner:

[Ex. 58]

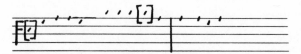

Caeli enarrant gloriam Dei   et opera manuum

Nam et servus tuus custodiet ea   in custodiendo illa

88 Tertius Modus:

[Ex. 59]

Magna est gloria eius in salutari tuo   *gloriam et magnum

Inueniatur manus tua omnibus inimicis tuis   *dex'tera tva   P 6v

89 Quartus Modvs:

[Ex. 60]

[F]

Non sunt loquelae neque sermones   *quorum non audiantvr

[F]

Hic accipiet benedictionem a Domino

*et misericordiam a Deo

Quoniam alieni insurrexerunt aduersum me et fortes quesierunt

animam meam   *et non proposuerunt

Ex. 59: e-ius P

Ex. 60: Non P W // loquele P // Hic P // (domino) et P

[88] Third Manner:

[Ex. 59]

Magna est gloria eius in salutari tuo   gloriam et magnum

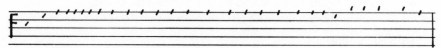

Inveniatur manus tua omnibus inimicis tuis   dextera tua

[89] Fourth Manner:

[Ex. 60]

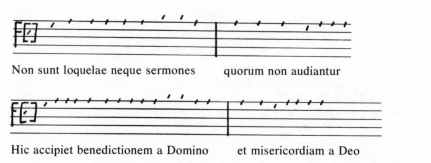

Non sunt loquelae neque sermones   quorum non audiantur

Hic accipiet benedictionem a Domino   et misericordiam a Deo

Quoniam alieni insurrexerunt adversum me et fortes quesierunt animam meam

et non proposuerunt

⁹⁰ Quintus **Modvs**:

[Ex. 61]

(neume notation)

Iusticiae Domini rectae laetificantes corda   *preceptum Domini

⁹¹ Sextus **Modus**:

[Ex. 62]

(neume notation)

Deus Deus meus respice [in] me   *quare me dereliquisti

⁹² QUINTUS TONUS

[Ex. 63]

(neume notation)

Gloria seculo-rum amen

(neume notation)

[A]   Soluite templum hoc

(neume notation)

Seculo-rum a-men

(neume notation)

[A]   Uox clamantis

Ex. 61: recte P // letificantes W

Ex. 62: Deus (Deus) P // Deus (Deus) W

Ex. 63: seculorum P W // Seculorum P W

⁹⁰ Fifth Manner:

[Ex. 61]

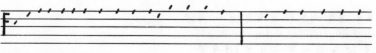

Iusticiae Domini rectae laetificantes corda   preceptum Domini

⁹¹ Sixth Manner:

[Ex. 62]

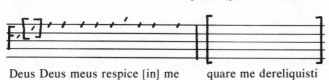

Deus Deus meus respice [in] me   quare me dereliquisti

⁹² FIFTH MODE

[Ex. 63]

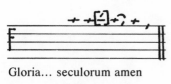

Gloria... seculorum amen

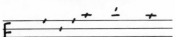

[A]   Solvite templum   hoc

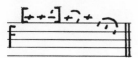

Seculorum amen

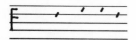

[A]   Vox clamantis

93 Psalmus:

[Ex. 64]

♪ ♪ ♪♪ ♪♪ ♪♪♪ ♪♪♪♪♪ ♪♪
Confitebor tibi Domine in toto corde meo

♪♪♪♪♪♪ ♪♪♪♪♪♪♪
*quoniam audisti uerba o-ris mei

♪♪♪♪♪♪ ♪♪
Adorabo ad templum sanctum tuum

♪♪♪♪♪   ♪♪♪♪♪♪
*et confitebor nomini tvo super misericordia tua et ueritate tva

♪♪♪
*qvoniam

          ♪♪♪♪♪   ♪♪♪♪♪
In quacumque die inuocauero te exaudi me   *multiplicabis

          ♪♪♪♪♪♪♪   ♪♪♪
Confitebor tibi Domine omnes reges terrae   *quoniam

          ♪♪♪♪♪♪   ♪♪♪
Quoniam magna est gloria Domini   *quoniam

Ex. 64: (tvo) Super W // (reges) terre W //

93 Psalm:

[Ex. 64]

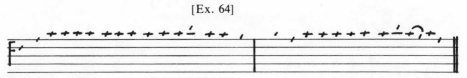

Confitebor tibi Domine in toto corde meo   quoniam audisti verba oris mei

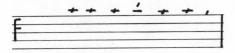

Adorabo ad templum sanctum tuum

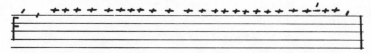

et confitebor nomini tuo super misericordia tua et veritate tua

quoniam

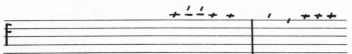

In quacumque die invocavero te exaudi me   multiplicabis

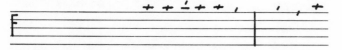

Confitebor tibi Domine omnes reges terrae   quoniam

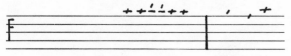

Quoniam magna est gloria Domini   quoniam

Si ambulabis in medio tribulationis uivificabis me

et super iram inimicorum meorum extendes manum tuam

*et saluum me fecit

Domine retribue pro me

*Domine misericordia tua in seculum

*et opera manuum

Dominus regnavit exultet terra   *laetentur [insulae]

Nubes et caligo in circuitu eius   *iusticiam et iudicium

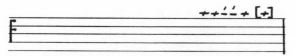

Si ambulabis in medio tribulationis vivificabis me

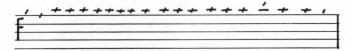

et super iram inimicorum meorum extendes manum tuam

et salvum me fecit

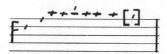

Domine retribue pro me

Domine misericordia tua in seculum

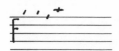

et opera manuum

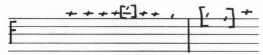

Dominus regnavit exultet terra   laetentur

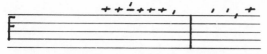

Nubes et caligo in circuitu eius   iusticiam

Ignis ante ipsum praecedet *et inflammauit

Illuxerunt fulgvra eius orbi terrae *vidit [et]

Montes sicut cera fluxerunt a facie Domini *a facie

Annuntiauerunt caeli iusticiam eius *et uiderunt omnes

Confundantur omnes qui adorant sculptilia *et qui gloriantur

Adorate' eum omnes angeli eius *audiuit [et]   P 7

Quoniam tu es Deus'altissimus super omnem terram   W 8

 *nimis [exaltatus]

Qui diligitis Dominum odite malum *custodit Dominus

Lux orta est iusto et rectis corde laeticia *laetamini

---

precedit P W // inflammauit P // (orbi) terre W // (a) facie P // celi W //

Adorate P W // custodite P // (corde) leticia P // letamini P W

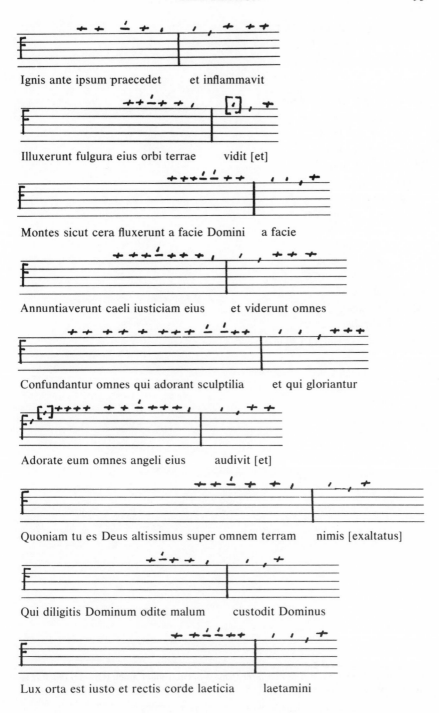

Ignis ante ipsum praecedet   et inflammavit

Illuxerunt fulgura eius orbi terrae   vidit [et]

Montes sicut cera fluxerunt a facie Domini   a facie

Annuntiaverunt caeli iusticiam eius   et viderunt omnes

Confundantur omnes qui adorant sculptilia   et qui gloriantur

Adorate eum omnes angeli eius   audivit [et]

Quoniam tu es Deus altissimus super omnem terram   nimis [exaltatus]

Qui diligitis Dominum odite malum   custodit Dominus

Lux orta est iusto et rectis corde laeticia   laetamini

94 DE TONO SEPTIMO

[Ex. 65]

♪ ♪ ♪ ♪ ♪ ♪ ♪ ♪
Gloria seculorum a-men

♪ ♪ ♪ ♪ ♪
[A]   Ora-bat Iudas

♪ ♪ ♪ ♪ ♪ ♪
Seculorum a-men

♪ ♪ ♪ ♪
[A]   Om- nes sitientes

♪ ♪ ♪ ♪ ♪ ♪
Secvlorum a-men

♪ ♪ ♪ ♪ ♪
[A]   Misit Dominus angelum

♪ ♪ ♪ ♪ ♪ ♪
Seculorum amen

♪ ♪ ♪ ♪
[A]   O-ran- te sancta Lucia

Ex. 65: Ora-bat P // *omnia inter* (Iudas) Seculorum *et* amen (Orante) *om* P // si-
cientes W

[94] SEVENTH MODE

[Ex. 65]

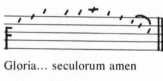

Gloria... seculorum amen

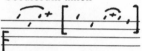

[A]   Orabat Iudas

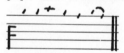

Seculorum amen

[A]   Om-nes sitientes[8]

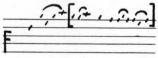

Seculorum amen

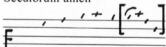

[A]   Misit Dominus angelum[9]

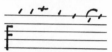

Seculorum amen

[A]   Orante sancta Lucia[10]

---

8   HARTKER, 18.
9   HARTKER, 281.
10   HARTKER, 26.

⁹⁵ [Psalmus:]

[Ex. 66]

(neume notation)
Be-nedictus Dominus Deus Israel

(neume notation)
*quia uisitauit et fecit redemptionem plebis suae

(neume notation)
Et erexit cornu salutis nobis   *in domo Dauid pueri sui

(neume notation)
Sicut locutus est per os sanctorvm   *[qui a seculo]

⁹⁶ DE TONO OCTAUO

[Ex. 67]

(neume notation)
Gloria seculo-rum amen

(neume notation)
[A]   Uenite post me

Ex. 66: quia uisitauit *s n* P // sue W // erexit P // sanctorum P

Ex. 67: Gloria seculorum amen *continuatim sub titulum priorem* P //

⁹⁵ [Psalm:]

[Ex. 66]

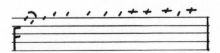

Benedictus Dominus Deus Israhel

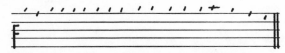

quia visitavit et fecit redemptionem plebis suae

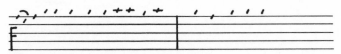

Et erexit cornu salutis nobis   in domo David pueri sui

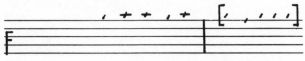

Sicut locutus est per os sanctorum   [qui a saeculo]

⁹⁶ EIGHTH MODE

[Ex. 67]

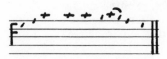

Gloria... seculorum amen

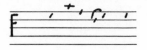

[A]   Venite post me

Seculorum amen

[A]   Omnes gen-tes per girum

[Seculorum amen]

[A]   Ho-die scie-tis

Seculorum amen

[A]   Propi-ci-us esto peccatis nostris Do-mi-ne

⁹⁷ Haec itaque, propter tardiores fratres, exempli causa congesta sunt abundantiore fortasse copia quam decuerit. ⁹⁸ Non frustra tamen si quis haec curat, nec superuacuae diligentiae obiurgat.

⁹⁹ 'Hoc uero admonendum quia quaedam non eiusdem   Bg 38v toni antiphonae indiscretam iniciorum similitudinem habent, ut in sequentiis cui melo quaeque aptanda sit uideatur, et maxime cuiusque cantus attendatur finis in quo cuiusque toni proprietas euidentius claret uerbi causa:

---

⁹⁹   *Titulus:* De laudis dei disciplina sermo Bg // ammonendum Bg // maximae P
gen-tes P // (scietis) Seculo-rum P // peccatis P // [Do-mi-ne] P

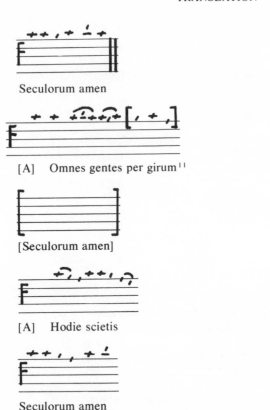

Seculorum amen

[A]   Omnes gentes per girum[11]

[Seculorum amen]

[A]   Hodie scietis

Seculorum amen

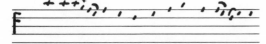

[A]   Propicius esto peccatis nostris Domine

[97] For the sake of the slower-witted brethren these illustrative examples have been amassed here perhaps more abundantly and at greater length than will be necessary. [98] But it will not be in vain if there is a single person to consult them and not reprove this over-diligence. [99] A word of caution: certain antiphons not belonging to the same mode have such similar beginnings that to continue one with the melody of the other would seem quite natural; special attention must be paid to the ending of each chant, where the indication of its mode appears most clearly. Example:

[11]   HARTKER, 354.

[Ex. 68]

[A]　A　bi-matu　et　in-fra　occidit　mul-tos　pueros　Hero-des

prop-ter Do-minum

[A]　Am-bu-labunt　mecum　in　al-bis　quoniam　digni　sunt　et　non

delebo nomina eo-rum de li-bro uitae

1 Hae quidem antiphonae simili principio ordiuntur sed' mox in processu discrepant et una secundi altera quarti toni melo deputanda apparet. *2* Similiter in multis. *3* Sunt etiam, ad quas canendi sunt psalmi, iuxta principalis melodiam cum subiugalis habeant finem. *4* Aut iuxta subiugalem modulentur et in principalem desin*a*nt. *5* Sunt qui non in finalem sonum terminantur sed in grauiorem qui sub se est. *6* Repetit autem neuma finalis illum in quo legitime cantus consistit et finit vt:'

P 7v

Bg 39

[Ex. 69]

[A]　Sci-mus　quoniam　diligenti-bus　Deum　omnia　co-o-pe-ran-tur

in bonum his qui secun-dum pro-po-si-tum uocati sunt

sanc-ti

4　desinent Bg P W
5　sunt <etiam> qui Bg // terminentur Bg
6　reppetit P

Ex. 68: *s n* Bg // al-bis P // uite W

Ex. 69: *s n* Bg // qui P // *neuma:*

P

[Ex. 68]

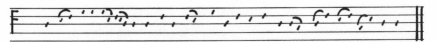

[A]   A bimatu et infra occidit multos pueros Herodes   propter Dominum

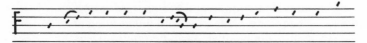

[A]   Ambulabunt mecum in albis quoniam digni sunt et non

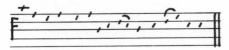

delebo nomina eorum de libro vitae

1 These antiphons do certainly begin alike, but thereafter in their continuation differ: the one clearly assignable to the second mode and the other to the fourth. *2* The situation is similar in many other cases. *3* Moreover, there are some antiphons, ones which require the singing of psalms, which combine an authentic melody with a plagal ending, *4* or which close in the authentic, having been sung in the plagal. *5* There are others which do not terminate with the *finalis*, but on a lower note. *6* The concluding melisma, however, returns ultimately to the note on which the chant legitimately comes to a close:

[Ex. 69]

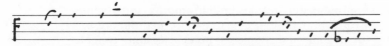

[A]   Scimus quoniam diligentibus Deum omnia cooperantur

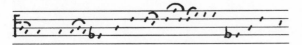

in bonum his qui secundum propositum vocati sunt

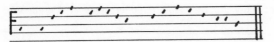

sancti

⁷ Sunt quaedam nothae [modulationes] ad quas psalmi proprio modo non aptantur, quae conferendo magis insinuari possunt.

⁸ De cetero ante omnia sollicitius obseruandum ut aequalitate diligenti cantilena promatur, qua utique si careat praecipuo' suo priuatur iure et legitima perfectione w 86v fraudatur. ⁹ Sine hac quippe chorus concentu confunditur dissono, nec cum aliis concorditer quilibet cantare potest nec solus docte. ¹⁰ Aequitate plane pulchritudinem omnem nec minus quae auditu quam quae uisu percipitur Deus auctor constare instituit, quia in mensura et pondere et numero cuncta disposuit.

¹¹ Inaequalitas ergo cantionis cantica sacra non uiciet, non per momenta neuma quaelibet aut sonus indecenter protendatur aut contrahatur, non per incuriam in vno cantv uerbi gratia responsorii uel ceterorum segnius quam'prius p 8 protrahi incipiatur. ¹² Item breuia quaeque imped*itios*iora non sint quam conueniat breuibus, nec longa inaequalitate lubrica festinantius labantur quam conueniat longis. ¹³ Uerum omnia longa aequaliter longa [sicut] breuium sit par breui-tas, exceptis distinctionibus quae [nihilominus] simili cautela in cantu obseruandae sunt. ¹⁴ Omnia quae diu ad ea quae non diu legitimis inter se morulis numerose concurrant et cantus quilibet totus eodem'celeritatis tenore Bg 39v a fine usque ad finem peregatur.

¹⁵ Hac tamen ratione seruata dum in cantu qui raptim canitur, circa finem aut aliquando circa initium longiori mora melos protendendum est. ¹⁶ Aut cantus qui morose canitur modis celerioribus finiendus ut pro modo breuitatis prolixitas prolongetur, et secundum moras longitvdinis momenta formentur breuia, ut nec maiore nec minore sed semper unum alterum duplo svperet. ¹⁷ Dum canente quolibet respondetur ab alio unum morositas seruent utrique modum, nec unus altero impeditiosius aut celerius canet.

---

⁷ quedam Bg W // modo: melo Bg
⁸ equalitate Bg W
⁹ quaelibet Bg
¹⁰ pulchritudine P W// quia: qui Bg // et numero *om* Bg // et numero: inbumero P
¹¹ inequalitas W // gracia Bg
¹² impeditiosiora: impendiora Bg // *omnia inter* breuibus *et* Uerum *om* P W // breuibus: longis Bg // longis: breuibus Bg
¹³ equaliter W
¹⁴ numerosae P
¹⁶ caelerioribus P

7 There are some spurious [intonations] which are not, properly speaking, suitable for the psalms, but which being assigned nonetheless have been able to insinuate themselves.

8 For the rest, there must above all be scrupulous regard that the chant is sung with strict evenness, for if this be lacking the chant is most certainly deprived of its special character and defrauded of its rightful and proper perfection. *9* Indeed, without it the singers are confused by the discordant effect, and none is able to sing in time with others nor even correctly alone. *10* God the creator has ordained that all beauty, no less when it is perceived through hearing than by sight, consists in unimpaired uniformity; for in measure, weight and number he has disposed of all things.

11 Unevenness of singing must not, therefore, be allowed to spoil the sacred chant; no note or neume is to be unduly quickened or retarded; neither may one be negligent and start to sing during a chant (a respond, for example, or any other piece) more slowly than at the beginning. *12* Another point: Breves must not be slower than is fitting for Breves; nor may Longs be distorted in erratic haste and made faster than is appropriate for Longs. *13* But just as all Breves are short so must all Longs be uniformly long, except at the divisions, which must [nevertheless] be sung with similar care. *14* All notes which are long must correspond rhythmically with those which are not long through their proper inherent durations, and any chant must be performed entirely, from one end to the other, according to this same rhythmic scheme. *15* In chant which is sung quickly this proportion is maintained even though the melody is slowed towards the end, or occasionally near the beginning (*16* as in chant which is sung slowly and concluded in a quicker manner), for the longer values consist of the shorter, and the shorter subsist in the longer, and in such a fashion that one has always twice the duration of the other, neither more nor less. *17* While singing, one choir is always answered by the other in the same tempo, and neither may sing faster or slower.

18 Hac pariter diligentia custodita, ut uoces in unum amborum coeant, nec qui succinit humilius uel celsius respondeat quam ille qui praecinit, sed quantum fieri valet haec dissonantia caueatur. *19* Siue eiusdem sint modi uoces ambae seu alia pro conuenientia aut necessitate mutanda, sint tamen prout seruari potest ambae aequisonae. *20* Modum autem eundem uocis dico donec in alteram transeat et in nouam mutetvr.

21 Preterea quemadmodum psalmi uel alia quaelibet melodia ad rationem causae uel temporis' pro paucitate P 8v uero seu multitudine cantorum celsius uel humilius canendi sunt, nec enim indifferenti altitudinis modo cantum cuiusque temporis modulari oportet, uerbi gratia matutina laeticia elatiore canore celebranda quam noctvrna sinaxis, at nocturna quidam uigilanter sed temperate. *22* Psalmi qui continuatim' cum suis antiphonis dicuntur ad uesperam Bg 40 dumtaxat quinque aut quatvor ad nocturnas sex uel tres, illi etiam qui ad matutinas deputati sunt, aut aequali elatione omnes imponendi aut certe a primo ad extremum melodia gradatim debet, et moderate in altum excrescere. *23* Cantica quoque euangelii altius et morosius ceteris, sicut inquam psalmis dicendis in efferendo et in submittendo ratio dictat modum. *24* Ita nihilominus quam producte uel correpte' dici oportet. *25* Uerum siue morosius siue celerius W 87 dicantur, hoc attendi semper debet ut honestis et plenis neumis congruo celeritatis pronuntientur modo ut nec nimiae protractionis tedeat, nec eos inreuerenti festinantia os ignobiliter canens ebulliat.

26 In pronuntiatione psalmorum cum antiphonis semper principia uersuum protendantur, una scilicet longa syllaba, longa autem pro modo correptionis quatinus chorus omnis pariter capere initia uersuum possit, et concorditer perducere. *27* Similiter uersuvm finis una uel duabus

---

18   amborum in unum Bg // precinit Bg
21   quelibet P W
21   multitodine *cor in* multitudine W // leticia W // elatiori Bg // aelatiore P // canorem P // At Bg P W // synaxys Bg
22   antiphanis *cor in* antiphonis W // elatione: eleuatione Bg // imponendi omnes Bg
23   sicut: Sciat P W // racio P
24   protractionis: protectionis P W
25   pronuncientur Bg
26   pronunciatione Bg
26   inicia Bg

18 Similar care is to be taken that the choirs keep to the unison, and that in responding neither joins in higher or lower than the other began, for this discord is to be avoided at all costs. *19* Now, if both choirs are singing at the same pitch, and one for convenience or out of necessity must change, then, as soon as possible, they must return to the unison. *20* This is the procedure for the choir whenever there is a change of pitch and a shift to a new level.

21 To continue, the psalms or any other melody ought to be sung at a high or low pitch depending upon conditions or circumstances, because, for instance, of having few or many singers; for the pitch at which a chant is sung is not a matter of indifference, but must suit the circumstances. To give another example, the morning office should be celebrated with joyful, higher-pitched singing than that for the night service, which should be performed in a lively manner but with decorum.

22 The psalms and antiphons sung in uninterrupted succession, namely the four or five at Vespers, the three or six at Nocturns, and those which are assigned to Lauds, should all be pitched at the same level; or at least should rise by degrees gradually in the course of the singing. *23* The Gospel Canticles, however, are to be sung at a higher pitch than the others and more slowly; for, as it is with regard to the heightening and lowering of the pitch in psalm-singing, so is it in the matter of singing slowly or quickly: the circumstances dictate the manner. *24* (In no case, however, is the singing to be too rapid or too slow.) *25* But whether slow or fast, care should be taken that the splendid long neumes are sung at a suitable speed; they should be neither tediously slow nor mouthed exuberantly in irreverent and vulgar haste.

26 In reciting psalms with antiphons, the beginnings of the verses are always prolonged (the first syllable alone lengthened, and only slightly) in order that the whole choir might begin the verses together and continue concordantly. *27* At the conclusion of the verses one or

productis' eadem longitudine syllabis, ut nec praeripiatur P 9
uersus sequens, praecedente nondum terminato nec rursus
intercapedo maior sit inter uersum et uersum quam finalium
syllabarum legitima longitudo.

[28] Repetitio antiphonarum quae in fine uersuum inter
captandum fit eadem qua psalmus celeritate percurrat,
porro finito psalmo legitima productione protendatur duplo
dumtaxat' longius. [29] Excepto dum cantica euangelica sic Bg 40v
morose psalluntur, ut non longiori, sed eadem morositate
antiphonam subsequi oporteat.

[30] Haec qualicumque de psalmorum melodiis et aequitate canendi prout potui de diuersis collecta descripsi, non
preiudicans illis qui easdem modulationes licet aliter non
minus tamen bene et fortasse melius habent. [31] Quae
canendi aequitas rithmus grece latine dicitur numerus,
quod certe omne melos more metri diligente mensurandum
sit.

[32] Hanc magistri scolarum studiose inculcare discenti-
bus debent, et ab initio infantes eadem aequalitatis siue
numerositatis disciplina informare. [33] Inter cantandum aliqua
pedum manuumue uel qualibet alia percussione numerum
instruere, ut a primeuo usu aequalium et inaequalium
distantia calleant, nec peiore usu assuescant. [34] Quorum
exercitiis haec pauca confeci cupiens eos laudis Dei
disciplinam nosse et cum supplici deuotione scienter Deo
obsequi.

---

[27] preripiatur Bg
[28] Repeticio P // finitimo P W // legitim[a] W
[30] Hec W // de *om* PW // equitate P W
[31] quod: quo Bg // m[e]tri P
[32] debet P W // inicio Bg
[33-34] *omnia inter* calle[...] *et* eos *om* P // deuocione P // hec W

two syllables are similarly lengthened so that the verse to follow will not anticipate the termination of the preceding, and so there will not be, on the other hand, between one verse and another (besides the legitimate lengthening of the final syllables) any letting up.

28 The repetitions of the antiphons which occur between the verses should be at the same speed as the psalms, but when the psalm is finished the antiphon is to be slowed by exactly half to its proper tempo. 29There is an exception in the case of the Gospel Canticles, which are sung so slowly that their antiphon should follow at the same tempo, and not be further protracted.

30 I have set down these observations on psalmody and evenness of singing borrowing, to the extent I was able, from diverse sources. But I do not prejudge those who quite permissibly sing the same intonations differently; their way is not worse and may perhaps be better, 31Singing performed with evenness is said to have "rithmus" [ρὑθμός, proportion] by the Greeks and "numerus" [measure] by the Latins, for without question all music should be strictly measured in the manner of prosody.

32 Teachers must impress this zealously upon their pupils, imparting to the children from the beginning this habit of evenness and strict measure. 33While they are singing the rhythm should be marked by the tapping of the foot or hand or whatever, so that from the start they will understand the difference between evenness and unevenness and not develop bad habits. 34It is for these pupils, to provide them with examples, that I have written this little work, wishing them to learn the discipline of the Divine Office and with humble service to praise God properly.

Commentary

The numbers refer to the text.

— 9 — *differentias* : This word has not, here, its technical meaning of "terminations." It is the eight modes which are under discussion, not the psalm tones.

quos ita nominamus : a reference, doubtless, to the controversy concerning the use of *tonus* in preference to *modus*. Chartier has assembled the principal medieval texts which discuss this matter (*La "Musica,"* see his Commentary).

— 10-15 — This passage (cf. *Scholia Enchiriadis*, GS I, 181) is based upon a very old text whose influence upon a number of ancient treatises has been studied by Huglo (*Les tonaires*, 47-55).

— 16 — This passage might at first suggest that the same psalm-tones were used for all chants, but it can only mean that all make use of psalm tones which reflect the structure of their mode. An elaborate psalmody for the Great Responsories is well-attested in the tenth century.

— 19 — *apud nos* : The melodies and syllables of the echematic formulas varied considerably from place to place. See BAILEY, *The Intonation Formulas*, *passim*.

— 22, Ex. 4 — The *initium* is unusal, and might be dismissed as a slip of the pen, but all the manuscripts agree, and even copyists unfamiliar with daseian signs could not fail to understand the notation of this example. (The version of M2 was almost certainly copied into a blank, and must not be considered a correction.) The figure is, moreover, repeated for the eighth tone.

— 25, Ex. 7 — The addition of the note to the melisma is supported by the consensus of sources for the echematic formulas. See BAILEY, *The Intonation Formulas*, 67.

— 26, Ex. 8 — The antiphon differs slightly in its two appearances. Cf. Ex. 56.

— 28, Ex. 10 — The *initium* is unusual, and possibly owing to a slip of the pen. But as in the case of Ex. 4, unanimity in the manuscripts gives it some claim to authority.

— 34, Ex. 16 — Please refer to the comments about Examples 4 and 10, above.

— 36 — *cantica euangeliorum* : the Magnificat and Benedictus.

— *cum ad hoc uacat* : It is not clear what this refers to.

— *quod superius expressum est* : The reference may be to the fact that all the antiphons cited in Examples 2-16 were for the Canticles.

— 37 — *ad cursum canendum*: for the psalter antiphons.

— 38 — *Noeane*: The *Commemoratio* probably read originally: *Noanoeane, etc.* The reading "Noane" was doubtless in the common source of Bg and W, the copyist of the former manuscript having corrected it without reference to the echematic formulas cited earlier in the treatise. Cf. *Musica Enchiriadis*, GS I, 158: *...utpote Noannoeane et Noeagis et caetera....* For the meaning of the echematic syllables see BAILEY, *The Intonation Formulas*, 20-26.

— 42, Ex. 20 — *custodiri*: The termination presumably begins at the second syllable. Cf. Ex. 56.

— 47 — There was some uncertainty in ancient books about the mode of antiphons of the *Benedicta tu* type. (Cf. REGINO OF PRÜM, GS I, 231.) See HUGLO, *Les tonaires*, 64 *et passim*, where, however, this scholar has inadvertently given the opening of the melisma as though it were the psalm tone.

— *Pronuntiet* is more correct grammatically than *pronuntiat*, and this is no doubt why Gerbert made the emendation (GS I, 217), but it seemed best to preserve the euphony of *pronuntiat-respondeat*.

— *alio modo respondeat*: It is clear from this remark that the semichoruses alternated complete psalm verses.

— 49, Ex. 27 — The emendation offered for this psalm tone should be compared with Ex. 48, where the same mediant cadence is found a fifth higher.

— 50, Ex. 28 — a version of the *Tonus Peregrinus*. It is not clear which is to be considered the reciting-note in the second half of this psalm tone. Cf. Huglo, *Les tonaires*, 395; Apel, *Gregorian Chant*, 213, 400. Ferretti, Apel and others have misunderstood "novissimus" (*Esthétique*, 310; *Gregorian Chant*, 213).

— 59, Ex. 35 — *scribentis*: The note for the first syllable may simply be a mistake. All of the terminations for the first tone in the *Commemoratio* descend from the reciting-note.

— 68, Ex. 43 — *uerba*: The termination evidently begins with the last syllable.

— 77-78 — It hardly seems necessary to include examples with musical notation to make this point. In any case, two vowels do not coincide at the caesura in the verses of Ex. 51. This section is, in fact, a supplement containing more examples of medians.

— 78, Ex. 51 — *sagitas suas*: the beginning of the next line of Psalm 7, and evidently copied inadvertently.

— 80 — The identity of the first and sixth tones, and the second and eighth, is a feature of the psalmody of the oldest books. Only in later times was the transition made from a six- to an eight-tone system. Modern scholars have tended to ignore the fact that there were originally fewer tones than modes.

— 82, Ex. 53 — *et colles*: Owing to the shortness of the second member the termination is begun immediately, without the accentual inflexion of the second-*initium* found in the other verses of this example.

— 83, Ex. 51 — *in seculum seculi*: This phrase, evidently copied inadvertently, is a version of the words *(in generatione et generationem)* which follow the previous psalm-verse (see Psalm 71). The words have been treated as a termination. The second appearance later is a simple case of dittography.

— *benedicent*: The versions of the psalms in the *Commemoratio* frequently differ from the standard. The Vulgate gives the close of Psalm 71 verse 15 as "tota die benedicent ei." The extra "benedicent" of this example was probably written reflexively by an inattentive copyist unaware that the version at hand terminated at an earlier point.

— *et misericordiam*: It is the need to start the termination immediately, and not any accentual considerations, which has necessitated the repeat of the *b* at the beginning of the second member of this verse.

— 85, Ex. 56 — The antiphon differs slightly from the version given in Ex. 8.

87, Ex. 58 — *illa*: The termination begins with the last syllable.

— *10* — Cf. Wisdom XI, 21: *sed omnia in mensura, et numero, et pondere disposuisti.*

— *15* — *circa initium*: Cf. *26.*

— *16* — *modis celerioribus finiendus*: If is difficult to imagine circumstances which require the quickening of a slow melody at the close. Gastoué *(Les origines*, 201, note 1) has suggested that the author has merely wished to include an elegant antithesis with the preceding phrase.

— *22* — The reference is to differences between the monastic and secular *cursus.*

— *25* — *honestis et plenis neumis*: the striking melismas of the Responsories, Graduals and Alleluias.

Glossary

Accentus: the position of the text-accent in relation to the central inflexion of the psalm-tone (71).

Aequalitas: rhythmic evenness (8).

Aequisonus: unison *(19)*.

Aequitas: rhythmic evenness *(30)* ; regularity, in the general sense *(10)*.

Brevis : a breve, a short note *(12)*.

Chorus: the semi-choir (47); all the singers *(9)*.

Cola: the juncture of the two members of a psalm-verse, the hiatus (78); from κόλλα? ; cf. *Musica Enchiriadis* (GS I, 182b): In colis vel commatibus... .

Distinctio: the division, the central inflexion of a psalm-tone, including the median cadence and second *initium (13)* ; Cf. *Guidonis Aretini Micrologus* (ed. J. Smits van Waesberghe [Rome, 1955], 163): ... distinctionem faciunt, id est congruum respirationis locum.

Elatio: level at which the singing is pitched *(21)*.

Excellentium (tetrachordum): the highest of the tetrachords (32).

Finalis (sonus): the final of the mode *(5)*.

Gravium (tetrachordum): the lowest of the tetrachords (22).

Inferior: the plagal form (73).

Longa: a long, a long note *(12)*.

Maiores antiphonas: the Mass antiphons (16).

Matutinae: Lauds *(21)*.

Medietas: the median, the central inflexion of a psalm-tone, including the median cadence and second *initium* (57).

Melodia: the psalm tone (37); the melodic structure (38); a chant *(3)*.

Melos: melodic structure regulated by tonal laws *(1)* ; melody (72).

Melos Dorium: a melody in one of the protus modes, i.e., modes 1 and 2 (72).

Membrum: a half-verse of a psalm (71).

Modulatio: the psalm intonation, the psalm tone (20).

Modus: manner (17).

Mora, morula: the duration of a note *(14, 15)*.

Neuma: the echematic formula (19); a melisma *(6)*.

Nothus: *(7)* cf. Regino: Sunt namque quaedam antiphonae, quas nothas, id est, degeneres et non-legitimas appellamus (GS I, 231).

Ordo (sonorum): the arrangement of the notes in a fixed series of tones and semitones (35).

Potius: the authentic form (74).

Sonus: a scale-step, a degree of the modal gamut (20). Cf. *Musica Enchiriadis*: Sonus quarumcumque generale est nomen (GS I, 159).

Superiorum (tetrachordum): the second-highest of the tetrachords (20).

Tenor (celeritatis): the rhythmic scheme, the fixed relationship of breves and longs *(14)*. Cf. *Aribonis de Musica* (ed. J. Smits van Waesberghe [Rome, 1951]), 67-68.

Terminalium (tetrachordum): the tetrachord comprising the four *finales* of the Gregorian modes (22).

Tonus: one of the eight Gregorian modes (9).

Vasa musicorum: undifferentiated musical instruments (6). Cf. J. Smits van Waesberghe, *Cymbala* (Bells in the Middle Ages) (Rome, 1951), 11.

Vox: the semi-chorus *(18)* ; the whole choir (20).

Appendix I

LIST OF ANTIPHONS CITED IN THE TREATISE

Modes designated in italics are not specified in the treatise. Asterisks indicate complete antiphons; all others are cues only. An obelus (†) indicates an interpolation or marginal addition. The sign # refers to the text outside the musical examples.

Antiphon	Mode	Location
*A bimatu et infra	2	Ex. 68
*Ambulabunt mecum	3	Ex. 68
*Anima mea exultabit	2	Ex. 27
Apertis thesauris suis (s n)	1	Ex. 32
*Benedicta tu in mulieribus	2	Ex. 25
Consurge consurge (s n)	2	Ex. 4†
Ecce nomen Domini	1	Ex. 30
Euge serue bone	1	Ex. 2, 31 (s n)
Ex Egypto uocaui (s n)	2	# 47
Hodie scietis	8	Ex. 67
*In templo Domini	8	Ex. 28
Innuebant patri eius	4	Ex. 56
Ioseph fili Dauid	7	Ex. 14
Laudabo Deum meum	4	Ex. 56
Magnum [haereditas]	2	Ex. 4
*Martyres Domini Dominum	8	Ex. 29
Misit Dominus angelum	7	Ex. 65
*Nos qui uiuimus	8	Ex. 29
*Notum fecit Dominus	6	Ex. 26
O quam (s n)	6	Ex. 12†
Omnes autem uos	4	Ex. 8, 56
Omnes gentes per girum	8	Ex. 67
Omnes sitientes	7	Ex. 65
Orabat Iudas	7	Ex. 65
Orante Sancta Lucia	7	Ex. 65
Paganorum multitudo	5	Ex. 10
Per uiscera misericordie	8	Ex. 16
Propicius esto peccatis	8	Ex. 67
Quando natus est	3	Ex. 52
Qui de terra est	3	Ex. 6
*Scimus quoniam diligentibus	1	Ex. 69
Sol et luna	1	Ex. 33
Soluite templum hoc	5	Ex. 63
Sub throno	7	Ex. 14†
Tu Betleem terra	3	Ex. 52
Uenite post me	8	Ex. 67
Uigilate animo	4	Ex. 56
Uox clamantis	5	Ex. 10†, 63

Appendix II

LIST OF PSALMS

An asterisk indicates that the verse in the *Commemoratio* differs from the standard version.

Example	Item	Psalm	Verse
Ex. 17	1	Psalm 118	1
Ex. 18	1		2
Ex. 19	1		3
Ex. 20	1		4
Ex. 21	1		5
Ex. 22	1		6
Ex. 23	1		7
Ex. 24	1		8
Ex. 26	1	Psalm 97	1*
	2		2*
	3		3
Ex. 27	1	Psalm 34	1
	2		2
	3		3
Ex. 28	1	Psalm 28	1
Ex. 34	1	Psalm 44	1
	2		3-4
	3		9*
Ex. 35	1		2
	2		5*
	3		8
Ex. 36	1		3
	2		7
Ex. 37	1		5
	2		6*
Ex. 38	1	Psalm 118	24*
Ex. 40	1	Psalm 18	3
	2		11
	3		14
	4		15
Ex. 41	1		2
	2		12*
	3	Psalm 108	8
Ex. 42	1	Psalm 20	6
	2		9
Ex. 43	1	Psalm 18	4*
	2	Psalm 53	5*
Ex. 44	1	Psalm 18	8*
	2		9

Ex. 45	1	Psalm 20	2
	2	Psalm 21	2*
Ex. 46	1	Psalm 7	5
Ex. 47	1		8-9*
Ex. 48	1	Psalm 17	2-3*
Ex. 49	1	Psalm 11	2
Ex. 50	1	Psalm 21	7
	2	Psalm 7	7
	3		7-8*
	4	Psalm 140	5*
Ex. 51	1	Psalm 7	8-9*
	2		13-14*
	3		16
	4		18*
Ex. 53	1	Psalm 71	2
	2		3
	3		4*
Ex. 54	1		4-5*
	2		6*
	3		15
	4		18-19*
	5	Psalm 23	5
Ex. 55	1	Psalm 71	9
	2		10
	3		13
Ex. 57	1	Psalm 18	3
	2		11*
	3		14
Ex. 58	1		2
	2		12*
Ex. 59	1	Psalm 20	6
	2		9
Ex. 60	1	Psalm 18	4
	2	Psalm 23	5
	3	Psalm 53	5
Ex. 61	1	Psalm 18	9
Ex. 62	1	Psalm 21	2*
Ex. 63	1	Psalm 137	1
	2		2
	3		3
	4		4*
	5		5-6
	6		7*
	7		8*
	8	Psalm 96	1
	9		2*
	10		3
	11		4
	12		5
	13		6
	14		7
	15		7-8
	16		9*
	17		10
	18		11-12

Appendix III

CHART OF THE ECHEMATIC FORMULAE FROM W

VII   No e a aae ane

V   No   e ane

III   Noea   noe   a   ne

I   No a no   e a ne

VIII   No e a gi

VI   No e a gi

IIII   No   e a gi[1]

II   No   e a gi

MIRA UIDES LECTOR IUNIORIS UERBA CATONIS
HAS COLE UIRTUTES SALUA SIT ALMA FIDES

---

[1]   The daseian symbols for the first part of the fourth-mode formula have been copied out of order in the manuscript:

No   e a gi.

BIBLIOGRAPHY

This list contains all books referred to in the Preface, Introduction and Commentary.

APEL, W., *Gregorian Chant*, Bloomington, 1958.

AUDA, A., *Les modes et les tons de la musique*, Brussels, 1931.

BAILEY, T., *The Intonation Formulas of Western Chant*, Toronto, 1974.

CHARTIER, Y., *La "Musica" d'Hucbald de Saint-Amand*, New York, Institute of Medieval Music, to appear in 1979.

COUSSEMAKER, E. de, *Mémoire sur Hucbald*, Paris, 1841.

FERRETTI, P., *Esthétique grégorienne*, Paris, 1938.

GASTOUÉ, A., *Les origines du chant romain*, Paris, 1907.

— "La psalmodie traditionnelle des huit tons," in the *Tribune de Saint-Gervais*, XIV (1908), 193.

GERBERT, M., *Scriptores Ecclesiastici de Musica Sacra Potissimum*, 3 vols, St.-Blasien, 1784.

HEINEMANN, O., *Die Handschriften der Herzoglichen Bibliothek zu Wolfenbüttel* IV, Wolfenbüttel, 1913.

HESBERT, R.-J., *Corpus Antiphonalium Officii*, 4 vols, Rome, 1963-70.

HUGLO, M., *Les tonaires*, Paris, 1971.

JAMES, M., *A Descriptive Catalogue of the Manuscripts in the Library of Corpus Christi College Cambridge*, 2 vols, Cambridge, 1911-12.

MOCQUEREAU, A., *Le nombre musical grégorien*, Tournai, 1908.

MÜLLER, H., *Hucbalds echte und unechte Schriften über Musik*, Leipzig, 1884.

MURRAY, G., *Gregorian Rhythm in the Gregorian Centuries*, Bath, 1957.

PETIT, (Abbé), *Dissertation sur la psalmodie*, Paris, 1855(?).

REESE, G., *Music in the Middle Ages*, New York, 1940.

SOLESMES (The Monks of), *Paléographie musicale*, Series 1: Vol. VII-VIII (1901), Cod. H. 159, Montpellier, Faculty of Medicine; Vol. XI (1912), Cod. 47 of Chartres. Series 2: Vol. I (new edition, 1970), Hartker's Antiphoner, St Gall MS 390-391.

— *La notation musicale des chants liturgiques latins*, 1960.

VOLLAERTS, J., *Rhythmic Proportions in Early Medieval Ecclesiastical Chant*, Leiden, 1958.

WAESBERGHE, J. Smits van, *Aribonis De Musica*, Rome, 1951.

— *Cymbala* (Bells in the Middle Ages), Rome, 1951.

— *Guidonis Aretini Micrologus*, American Institute of Musicology, 1955.

— *The Thoery of Music* (RISM), Munich, 1961.

WAGNER, P., *Einführung in die gregorianischen Melodien*, Leipzig, 1911.

Printed by les Éditions Marquis Ltée, Montmagny, Québec.